revelations

in the rearview mirror

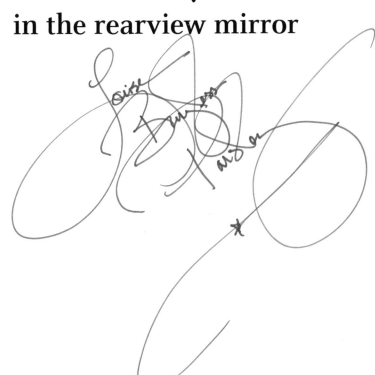

bright sky press

2365 Rice Blvd., Suite 202 Houston, Texas 77005

10 9 8 7 6 5 4 3 2 1

Library of Congress Cataloging-in-Publication Data

Parsley, Louise, 1955-
Revelations in the rearview mirror : reflections of a late-blooming mother / by Louise Parsley.
p. cm.
ISBN 978-1-933979-32-8 (alk. paper)
1. Motherhood–Humor. I. Title.

PN6231.M68P37 2009
306.874′3–dc22

2009000330

Book and cover design by Cregan Design, Ellen Peeples Cregan and Hina Hussein
Jacket photo by Karen Sachar Photography
Edited by Nora and Al Shire
Illustrations by Carroll Kempner Goldstone
Printed in China through Asia Pacific Offset

one mother's hard-won and hilarious epiphanies
on the road to the empty nest

in the rearview mirror

LOUISE PARSLEY

bright sky press
HOUSTON, TEXAS

www.brightskypress.com

My writing career began focused on my kids, and I suppose my future will be the same—although now from the vantage point of surviving the experience. As my children stepped further into their own journeys, I began stepping beyond their stories, outside the bubble of our charmed lives and into the community—first, volunteering, then speaking. Time and time again, I found myself drawn to pediatric oncology patients at various agencies.

Befriending these everyday angels, I became spellbound, soaking up the wisdom of their young souls that was well beyond their years. I observed goodness in dark places and even witnessed miracles. Beholding these small patients' special brand of courage as they sought peace through creativity, I felt them touch greatness. In touching greatness, they inspired those around them—doctors, nurses, their families, other patients...certainly, this writer—to reach harder for greatness.

Reflecting on many of my inadequacies as a mother, I often wonder with my own kids, just who raised whom? This bizarre role reversal is often experienced by parents sick with worry over their kids with cancer. Often, it is the child who teaches the parent not to be overcome by despair, fear or anger, and leads them to find new meaning to life.

Faith did that for me. I met her when she was four years old. A petite, beautiful child with soft, dark curls and enormous doe eyes framed with eyelashes so thick that I thought it surely must take extraordinary effort for her even to blink. On our path to friendship, we colored a little, talked a little and giggled with glee when we discovered that our birthdays were one day apart.

One day, gripping chunky Crayons, drawing fluffy clouds, lopsided flowers and her house under a giant rainbow, I asked Faith why she thought she had cancer—what was the purpose of it.

"Oh, that's easy," Faith replied, concentrating on her grass. "God puts you here to learn things, but He made me pretty perfect. I already know a lot." And without batting one enormous eyelash, she added, "So, I probably won't have to stay here very long."

"What about your parents?" I asked. Eyes widened, she answered, "Oh, they'll be here for a very long time. They have a LOT to left to learn."

Over the next two years, Faith drew me pictures that her mother would mail to me. And I sent Faith my Christmas letter and card with my family picture. We always remained connected through our "art."

I realized that I was unable to change the cards life had dealt these young patients, and each time we parted company I was challenged to find appropriate ways to honor their journey. I finally came to understand that the greatest homage I could pay them would be to savor my own kids, to appreciate and celebrate the time I have with them. To laugh with them...and even to cry with them.

One impossibly hot and steamy August morning, I boarded a chartered bus bound for Louisiana. With nothing to read, I found one lone section of the newspaper under my seat. The obituaries. There, from the far left column, that precious face with those doe eyes looked out...stopping my heart.

At Faith's service, I stood over the little one whose soul embodied her name. Unaware of the woman behind me, I felt a hand take mine—Faith's mother. She whispered, "Faith said you would come."

Faith. Indeed.

I have been blessed to befriend other patients, many through the Children's Cancer Hospital at the University of Texas M. D. Anderson Cancer Center. For those of you who have had, like me, only children who wanted to be carried, not ones who must, the spirit that lies within the kids at M. D. Anderson Cancer Center is a poignant reminder to live each day, to begin each day with hope...and to embrace the transforming power of love. Two pictures next to my computer serve as a reminder to me everyday. One, a drawing of a rainbow; the other, a photograph of Faith.

Ines, a patient at M. D. Anderson Cancer Center, created this heart through the hospital's Children's Art Project. It embodies the message of love, hope, faith... certainly, motherhood. May it serve as a reminder of all things powerful in this world—in particular, the magic you cannot see, but can only feel. I hope that, in some small way, this book will carry the love I breathed in from kids like Ines and Faith, as well as from my own, out further into the world.

Louise Parsley

To Elizabeth, Bayless and Garland—
for helping to uncover the best part of me—
And The Bob,
the best sport, husband and father
a wife could hope for

TABLE OF CONTENTS

Table of Contents

Introduction

Having been a traveler down the road of motherhood for 26 years, my college fascination with Kierkegaard's philosophy suddenly rose up to haunt me. "Life can only be understood backward, but it must be lived forward." Those words, in fact, have never rung truer.

With each blunder, flub and goof-up I have made on this journey, one thought continually rested on my shoulder—I am anything but a natural.

Standing at the back of the crowded line marked "Nurturing," I came away, shall I say, slightly empty-handed. As the first in line for "Cynicism/Idealism," I was doused mightily.

As my father would say, "Supply and demand." High demand, low supply. Low demand, you get drenched.

After a few missteps—including a larger-than-usual collection of engagement rings I found a real gem. Shortly after saying, "I do," we did. And we have been pursuing "happily"— with three kids joining our dream team—"ever after."

In the wee, small hours reserved for me, when the kids weren't looking—absorbed in their "all about me" world, their hair, *The Simpsons* or who dumped whom—I pushed to find a piece of the world for me. I spent time with those less fortunate, took in stray animals and kids, and wrote notes of encouragement to those in need of a friend.

In the examen of my life, I began to write, focusing on the thin line between laughter and pain, the challenges of kids and the tragedy of owning goldfish. And I found humor in strange places.

The only way I knew I was making any headway was not in my advancing steps, but seeing the distance I had come as I looked back in my rearview mirror. Tender mercy got me through the misfires of overreacting—handing down a life sentence to my son who spilled milk on our first "real" fake Oriental rug or getting out the bazooka to kill a gnat when my daughter ripped a hole in her pink tights and couldn't find her ballet shoes minutes before her recital. She was five years old.

Armed with faith that the road, if not a map, would always be there, I gave in to hindsight—it not only propelled me forward, but also taught me to breathe. By my third child, I was able to string together enough loud breaths to qualify as a laugh. Those laughs turned into columns. And some of those columns turned into this book.

While the writing of these stories was done over ten years, the material covers a span of over twenty-two years, beginning with my wedding, traverses across labor pains, tromps through their childhoods and adolescence, capping with my eldest leaving the nest for the real world. Funny, as she worked to find a job, I found—to my great surprise—that I'd worked myself out of one.

Rising to the challenge of having a mother who writes about every embarrassing thing they've ever done, my kids were far better sports than I ever could be. Writing might be my therapy, but it definitely will be the cause of theirs.

Yet, somewhere between setting boundaries and finding forgiveness we learned together that, laughing at ourselves, humor is the glue that holds us together.

As our dirty laundry was aired, our stories seemed to resonate with readers. Today, I might be at a lunch or cocktail party (but only if I can find shoes that match), and inevitably someone will say, "I still have the one about Little League/your dad's handkerchief/your son's car being the source of the ozone hole on my refrigerator door."

After all these years...

Little did I know at the time I was writing these stories that the eye-opening I experienced tapping into their hearts and finding the laughter would pale in comparison to the insight I have now looking back...still moving forward.

Reliving the endlessly loud late nights, the lectures over spilled milk (literally), the blind stabs at mothering, saying the wrong thing at the right time, even the slam-dunk "givens," in the end, it was the laughter—if and when we finally hit upon a punch line—that made it all so memorable.

Writing morphed into public speaking, which, as my life goes, is the No. 1 public fear in America. Fear of death is No. 2. In the beginning, standing before a crowd of two, I managed to combine Fear No. 1 and Fear No. 2, forget to breathe and fall into a pretty convincing state of rigor mortis.

Laughter, I realized, was even more important when directed at myself. Given the amazing amount of material I have on that very subject, that insight has served me well.

I have had the honor of speaking to a variety of groups about childhood cancer, Alzheimer's, heart disease, inner-city schools, at-risk youths...even the Gynecological and Obstetrical Society. As a result of educating myself and raising awareness in those around me, these causes became dear to my heart. But the challenge when speaking on these topics was finding humor in such serious invasions of our existence.

If you are not a woman, you must trust me that, when standing in front of 500 Ob-Gyns, the term "invasion" definitely crosses one's mind.

But time and time again, laughter bubbled up from those who were, many times, struck the deepest. The patients. The kids. The victims. Much like a gift wrapped in barbed wire, telling their stories not only illuminated lives and warmed audiences' hearts, but it also gave us permission to cry—tears of laughter blending with tears of pain. But nothing compared with those tears embodying the most glorious, exceptional human virtue.

Hope.

Other than trying to make sense of life's tragedies, nowhere does hope do more to bolster one's armor than being a mother. Unless it's being a writer.

I fell into motherhood, not by accident, but more the way one might fall apart, into enemy hands or to their knees praying for help.

As luck would have it, it was these same sensations I experienced as I fell into writing...which was a complete and total accident. Most days, it was a fourteen-car pileup; others, just a fender bender. Regardless of whom I wanted to blame, I could not dispute the fact that I was the one behind the wheel.

One of these professions alone—motherhood or writing—was enough to launch me into thin air, the upshot being plenty of hard landings. But, together, they simultaneously quieted and amplified my internal voice, allowing me to tap into pieces of me I did not know existed. Together, these pursuits excavated my spirit. Cutting through unnecessary top layers, my humanity was unearthed—and became illuminated.

Accident or destiny, both of these blessings were gifts from God.

As a little girl, being a mom was never part of my make-believe world. I never dragged a doll around by one foot, wondered why Barbie didn't have stretch marks, or burn the crumpets at a tea party. I was too busy pretending to be Eloise at The Plaza, dreaming of Kookie on 77 Sunset Strip and hoping to grow big enough to beat up my older brother. He had it coming—he slung me once by my ankles across the wooden floor and slammed my head into the foot of the bed. This, I explain to anyone who will listen, is why I never became the Pulitzer prize winner/supermodel/Secretary of State that I was destined to be.

I was, what my mother called, a late bloomer.

I wore corrective shoes through the eighth grade. I got a bra only to fill the requirement for high school gym, and experienced my first kiss when I volunteered to be the dummy in CPR class. And I didn't even get my period until I was old enough to vote. Now, it won't go away.

It might help you to know that my mother was perfect, always doing the right thing throughout her life. She was a talented dancer, quarterback of her college powder puff team, and a community superstar. When I had measles, she had our maid care for me, so she could volunteer at the children's hospital...to care for other children whom, she said, were really sick. It came as a huge surprise to her when I snuck out of the house at age sixteen to go to a fraternity party and was too sick the next day to even sit down at the family table for Sunday lunch. I still can't look at roast beef sandwiches without recalling Wild Turkey mixed with strawberry soda.

I know.

My father, who had no real father figure of his own, turned out to be the father of all time. Ignoring my obvious allergy to roast beef, he simply bided his time, praying that one day I'd figure out whether I was fish or fowl. Even when I dated loser after loser, he would simply turn to my mother and give her the sign to pray for rain...again. And rain it did. Building an emotional ark to sail me through a deluge of mistakes and floods of tears, he patiently waited for me to grow up.

Through sheer force of nature, I did grow up. Hard as I tried, I never did become Eloise or beat up my brother. And I'm still unsure whether I am fish or fowl. But once I finally accepted the fact that Zorro was not an option, I managed to find The Bob, the man for me. And what a man he is.

The only instruction my father ever offered about parenthood was this: "Children need boundaries." He died two and a half months before our first child, his first grandchild, was born—his loss, the greatest void of my life.

On our first Christmas Day as husband and wife, I delivered—and received—the gift of all gifts. No return, no exchange, no refund (trust me, I looked)—a baby girl.

As my O.B. handed this precious, pink bundle to me, it slowly dawned on me what being a late bloomer really meant. Instead of feeling I'd been found, I felt I'd been found out. If only I'd been more laid-back in that "Nurturing" line and not been in such a rush to be first in the "Cynicism" line.

Unfortunately, to do so would require patience, which is—and this came as a real shocker to me—a prerequisite for nurturing.

Before our second anniversary, I had a son. Almost eight years later, a third child, a daughter. Given the mistakes I'd made raising the first two, I embraced her as another chance—she was my last shot at redemption, my last pitch for perfection as a mom.

Nothing about caring for my children came instinctively. Giving birth was not the "Aha!" moment my friends had described. Neither a flash of clarity nor a light bulb going off, mine was more like a power surge of electricity in my brain that produced, instead of Eureka!, a migraine.

With no internal tour guide directing me how to parent, no map on how to get them to my end game, no one to call in Manila for technical support, these poor, defenseless babies were left in my care.

And I feared I was wired with the maternal warmth of Mommie Dearest.

Bedraggled and rough-feathered, I looked like a mother and quacked like a mother, so everyone, especially my children, believed I was a real mother. But looking back, I didn't realize in my haste and lack of living in the moment that I was wishing away their youths. I longed for the day they would be able to put themselves to bed, drive, bounce their own checks... blossom. All the while praying in devout silence that, as their mother, I would, as well.

All I could do was hold on for the ride. But hold on to what, was the question.

Holding On

Oh, the things I did not know as a new mother.

I did not know that when my breasts felt as though a two-ton gorilla was sitting on them, it was my milk coming in. And later, that the hair clogging the drains was not the gorilla's, but mine. I did not know that gremlins would hijack my hormones. Or that my multiple personalities would host a reunion...and not invite the real me. I felt as though entire conventions of mothers had been given the key to the secret of successful mothering, but when it was my turn, the keys were on back-order.

So many secrets that no one had ever shared...

With only my gut in control, I believed that my assignment was to raise a productive human being. But as I listened to Other Mothers, the first requirement for being a good mother was revealed: compare my child to every other child.

Let the games begin!

Consumer ratings began with APGAR scores in the delivery

room. My friends boasted that their babies scored perfect tens. Mine got sevens. I had not even made it into recovery, and I was making a C- in mothering.

Other Babies were potty-trained before my firstborn had bared her teeth. Other Babies walked at eight months. Mine fell off the kitchen counter while strapped in her infant seat, doing a face plant on the linoleum floor. At last, a ten.

Other Babies ate pulverized Brussels sprouts and gulped down 2.5 glasses of Soy milk daily. My son ate his weight in mud-covered rocks while my daughter drank 2.5 ounces of straight scotch (it's a long story, but let's just say it looks like apple juice). Luckily, she was fourteen...months.

Still saturated in cynicism and idealism, my gut refused to allow me to stand in line at 4 a.m. to register my toddlers in T.H.E. Mother's Day Out program that was their blueprint to success. My gut wouldn't allow me to mail—from the delivery room—my daughter's first year's rent for T.H.E. private college dorm. Or sign them up for T.H.E. summer camp. Oh, my poor kids started off at such a disadvantage.

My pre-school days were consumed with listening to Other Mothers tell tales of their toddlers tying their shoelaces in real bows, playing the piano by ear and reciting the Periodic Table. My kids were mouth-breathers, couldn't manage to stick two strips of Velcro together and bonded with imaginary friends who were, apparently, out on parole.

Other Mothers chaired the elementary school play, the auction and hired professionals to manage their campaign for Room Mother of the Year. I locked my third baby inside my car with the engine running in front of God and Payless Shoe Store.

Other Mothers looked on and simply shook their heads in pity...then did a dance in the end zone celebrating their own victory as a mother.

Enduring the endless attempts to teach manners (no shooting peas out of your nose until *after* dinner), family car trips (playing rock-paper-scissors to determine who would get strapped to the roof), reading their tear-stained letters from camp—or, worse, receiving no camp letters at all—I kept my eye on the future, believing that perhaps my children would prevail in spite of me and dreaming of easier times to come.

As payoff in the genetic roulette wheel, each child brought into my life a different set of concerns.

My eldest, audibly quiet, was demure, timid and shy as a violet. Her enormous brown eyes would take in the world, looking up to me for guidance. I worried she would never have an opinion or stand on her own.

Her brother, born with a furrowed brow and overdeveloped sense of purpose, oozed passion with his overwhelming personality. I worried he would never stand down.

The youngest bounced into our lives out of nowhere. Her glass overflowing with positive energy, she managed, somehow, to stay in perfect balance. With an affable smile and gracious charm, she was born for the world to enjoy. My only concern about her was—could she really have come from me?

As ill-equipped as I was—substituting sweetened condensed milk for formula, never having a Kleenex for green noses or enough Benadryl to sedate me through 9,756 stanzas of Mr. Rogers' "Won't you be my neighbor?"—little did I know these days would be a stroll down *Sesame Street*.

In these early years, I had no idea I'd ever have to wash the bar of soap before taking a bath or need a sandblaster to remove the algae from my kids' unbrushed teeth or Sharpie scribbling from my walls.

I had no idea I'd have to hold on for dear life the first time they crossed the street, rode a bike, made an oatmeal volcano for the Science Fair that really could erupt—and did, all over my hair, face and kitchen.

I had no idea how much my six-year-old son would hate

me for making him walk by himself to the police department ten blocks away to report his stolen bike—the one I'd warned him nine gazillion times not to leave outside. Unlocked. Or the debilitating fear that would run through my daughters' veins when I made one confess to her teacher that she'd forged my signature on a test and the other return a friend's coveted hair band that she'd borrowed...permanently.

And none of my children had any idea how much character it took for each of them to rise to those challenges.

Each night as I tucked them in before I lay me down to sleep, I prayed to become a better mother. Since a real mother refused to show up at our house, I wondered...couldn't I just hire one? Buy the supersecret ingredients via catalog? Or in bulk at Sam's Club?

What criteria did it take to be a good mother? If it was patience, I was a dead woman. If it was the ability to simultaneously make costumes with dryer lint and sandwiches with homemade bread and not confuse the two; or communicate at a low-enough decibel not to shatter the stemware, I was doomed.

But if it was heart—

a heart that cracked the first time I put them on the bus to camp;

a heart that is silenced as they figure out on their own that their new boyfriend is a juvenile delinquent, or girlfriend a man-eater;

a heart strong enough to make them earn their own money, do their own laundry and clean their room... when it was so much easier for me to do it;

a heart that could expand with each kiss lovingly bestowed on their foreheads as they lay sleeping and turn to mush as I unwrapped yet another clay handprint on Mother's Day; and a heart that could teach them to share their gifts, live with failure, help them find what sutains them from the inside, be true to themselves and see beauty on days when it is anything but.

If being a good mother took a heart that could do all those things, then maybe I had a reasonable shot. "Mother of the Year," never. But maybe not the woman who birthed the Unabomber, either.

Pearl of Great Price

When I was a little kid, my dad gave me two pieces of advice: "Elope" and "Marry an orphan."

Dad was a smart guy. He had done his math on the cost of throwing a Barbie-type wedding, and Chapter 11 was not in his book. If I did not elope, then at least marrying an orphan would seriously reduce the amount of clam dip at the reception.

When I brought home The Bob, a guy who is the oldest of ten kids, with an extended family of nearly 80, there was not enough Pepto-Bismol in all the drugstores in Houston for Dad to swill.

"Did you look in the trunk of his car?" Dad bellowed. "His lunch from seventh grade is in there. And an old jockstrap that looks like a Chia Pet."

"But, Dad, we are both left-handed." To the President of Perfection, we were a disaster area.

On the big day, the Hatfields and McCoys agreed to leave their shotguns at home. I do not remember much, because my gown was so tight it cut off the circulation to my brain. With gown was so tight it cut off the circulation to my brain. With only two hours of sleep, I looked just like my driver's license picture. My face was the same color as my gown. Antique white. My attitude was old, my shoes new, my padded bra borrowed, and my lips blue.

As Dad steered me down the aisle, a Gang of Seven was standing at the altar: four priests, a minister, a rabbi and a televangelist brought in to close the deal. To the right, stood the man I had known only ten months whose idea of Big R Romance was asking me to caddy for him.

Dad saw a guy who had never done his own laundry, used Hefty trash bags as luggage, and who correlated all aspects of his life to sports.

I saw the promise of adventure.

The officials looked over their half-glasses and down their collective noses at us and boomed, "Who gives this woman to be married to this man?" Light-headed from counting fleeing dollar signs, my father replied, "First City National Bank... and me."

One of the priests stepped forward in about the third quarter. His baritone voice in the great hall as it bounced off the church's stone floor and ricocheted off the stained glass. My bouquet and my bones shook. With great passion, he spoke of the slimy, dirty oyster lying in the cold darkness at the bottom of the sea. As the oyster skims the ocean floor, it consumes a tiny grain of sand, which rubs and chafes the mollusk's body muscle. The more the oyster writhes inside its hard, ugly shell trying to rid itself of the irritating grain of sand, the greater the irritation becomes. In self-defense, the oyster creates a protective coating around the sand. Then one day, the oyster produces a pearl.

As he became more consumed with the plight of the oyster, his voice sank deeper and deeper. And so did I.

Suddenly, he quickly announced, "I now pronounce you

husband and wife. Amen."

At this point I retreated into my inner thoughts, which went something like "Wha?" This was no Barbie wedding ceremony. It was a death sentence to the holy state of acrimony. I knew I could be as irritating as any grain of sand inside some slimy, dirty, ugly oyster, but hey, let's be fair. So could the groom.

With that, the trumpets sounded, The Bob high-fived me and off we went, retreating down the aisle to the tune of "Can This Marriage Be Saved?"

Reality hit in the limo. I had spent six months focusing on a wedding, not a marriage. And certainly not some slimy oyster. We had not even discussed a warranty. What if I could not mold him into the guy I wanted in ninety days?

There is nothing like kids, a mortgage and a midlife career change to understand the oyster and the great price it pays for its pearl. It is a daily rub to live with a guy who falls asleep with the TV on, uses all the hot water, and is always twenty minutes late. Many days, love is neither patient nor kind.

Marriage is enduring thousands of days of irritation, as well as the numbing madness of routine and the undeniable responsibility to one another. But, by enduring the rub, we create the pearl of love and acceptance.

Of course, being a pretty good caddy helps. Not to mention being left-handed.

No return, No Exchange

The holiday season. Technically, this joyous season should not begin until the kitchen is cleaned from the turkey massacre on Thanksgiving Day. Yet, today's Christmas kickoff falls closer to Labor Day, when the Neiman Marcus catalog arrives. By Halloween, I'm humming "Jingle Bells" subconsciously with the organ player in the grocery store. By Thanksgiving, my credit cards have melted.

This time of year brings out the best in me...on par with Scrooge. I love the river of humanity that floods the streets, the rat race at the shopping malls, and the Grinches who steal parking spaces. I can hardly wait for our annual family brawl over which Christmas tree to buy. The 90-degree temperature in the shade always adds to the spirit. And how I look forward to my favorite bonding moment—the family Christmas card photo. Our photographer now comes dressed as a referee, armed with a cattle prod and Mace.

There are school plays, breakfast with Santa, ballet recitals, office parties, lunch with Santa, 101 trips to the hardware store for extension cords and light fuses, and, of course, the smell of Santa's cookies burning. Our immediate families (last count: 83 1/2), who consider every meal their last, will gather together three different times...at our house. I have 21 shopping days left, a list of 143 gifts, and I'm exhausted. It could only get worse if I wake up as Martha Stewart.

As this Season of Peace spins wildly out of control, it is no wonder families try to focus on the spiritual aspect of the holidays. The only rest I get is sitting in church.

Trying to reflect on the heart of the season, I asked my children the meaning of Christmas. My kindergartner said it was when three wide guys crossed the sandpile and found baby Jesus, who is like a Power Ranger, but better. They brought the baby gold, frankfurters and a mirror.

Her elder brother added that there were these wise guys from the East Side who thumbed across the desert and found baby Jesus wrapped in waddling clothes with his manager.

My teenager, with the clarity innate to all firstborn children, said the urchin Mary had an immaculate contraction. Then she asked if I knew where Joseph bought his amazing Technicolor dreamcoat. Whatever.

Each Christmas, I recall my own immaculate conception as my family celebrates not only the fruit of Mary's labor pains, but also the birth of our first child.

Although I had carried that little bundle around like Santa's fanny pack for nine months, the warning signs of her impending arrival still came as a surprise at 11:30 p.m. Christmas Eve. Always one to make a big entrance, this child punched a hole the size of my fist through the wall of its water-filled cocoon, right in the middle of Midnight Mass. With little warning, I—and the once-close family members sitting next to me—felt as if we had been thrust down the log ride at Jungle Surf.

And so, Christmas morning, while the rest of the world was counting presents under their tree, I was doing deep breathing amidst a bunch of animals in the delivery room. Just like Mary. My husband had one eye on me and one eye on the TV in the opposite corner of the room, watching the Sun Bowl. The score, he reported excitedly, was tied.

I was enthralled.

With three seconds left in the game, Longhorns 4th and goal, it happened.

We became a family.

The nurse handed me our tiny, squirming package, bundled up in a Christmas stocking. I looked in awe at her miraculous little hands and counted her toes again and again. Fearful of breaking her, I gently handed the baby to her dad. Even through his blurred vision, he saw a dream. I saw love at first sight. Taking turns holding this most precious Christmas gift, we knew our lives would never be the same.

The dashing, dancing and prancing, once reserved for only the holiday season, is now what we do daily. Some days better than others. Each year on Christmas Day, after the gifts have been opened, the turkey devoured and the last of the cousins has retreated because we ran out of wine, we retell the story of Christmas and what it means to each of us. We light the growing number of candles on her cake and talk about the best gift ever. The gift that keeps on giving. At last, after weeks of our hearts racing wild with anticipation and excitement, a modicum of peace and calm is restored.

This season is about family. And friends. And exhaustion.

It doesn't get any better than that.

Sufferin' Succotash

There's a basic tenet to raising children that is incontrovertible, yet parents refuse to accept it. Kids hate to eat anything good for them. When mine were babies, I'd retreat from the high chair looking like Regan's mother in *The Exorcist* with strained peas in my hair, watching in horror as they jettisoned Vienna sausages into the neighbor's pool.

By the age of reason (which should be raised 70 years), they became magicians, making vegetables mysteriously disappear by dissecting them into tiny microbes and rearranging them on the plate, hiding chunks under the seat cushion and shoveling large amounts into their napkin which they would later stamp and mail to their aunt in New Jersey.

"I don't like Brussels sprouts," they sneered.

"How do you know? You've never had one. Just take a bite.

It won't kill you," I'd say lovingly through gritted teeth.

"Oh, yeah? That's what Eve said to Adam, and look what a stir that caused."

It had to have been a mom who gave birth to the first food fight, heaving fistfuls of mashed potatoes at her malnourished children, hoping to force-feed them through their windpipes.

My generation wasn't any better. As a kid, I spilled a glass of milk every night at the dinner table, hoping to avoid eating anything with nutritional value. While Dad said the blessing, I prayed it would be my last supper. I suffered through succotash, barfed over broccoli and gagged at green beans. But I couldn't leave the table until I had either cleaned my plate, it was time to go to school, or the food had a moustache. I didn't care how many starving Armenian children I killed, maimed or injured by not eating lima beans. They just lay there limp, lame and anemic, the life steamed out of them. No sauce, no dressing, just nuked and nude.

My husband grew up with nine siblings and a mom who knew how to cook. She would slather food with sauces, use real butter and sprinkle an extra dose of salt. She'd let the kids put ketchup on their corn, mustard on their greens, and molasses on carrots. They still wouldn't eat. Dinner was on the table at 3:30, sharp. If the Tazmanian Ten hadn't finished by 7:00 p.m., she'd set the kitchen timer for 2 hours. If they still hadn't finished, she'd take up their plates, save the leftovers and feed it to them for breakfast—in addition to their real breakfast.

It was the birth of eating disorders.

As a newlywed, I fixed my husband our first meal.

"What's that?"

"Spinach."

"Why is it green? Mom's spinach was never green."

"That's because she cooked it in motor oil and covered it with eggs to fulfill your minimum daily requirement of cholesterol."

"At least cholesterol is low in fat and doesn't make you pucker." This from a man who melts a pound of butter in the skillet before frying bacon, thinks fat grams are a basic food group, and says that together we make an average-size couple.

By the time my last food critic was born, I'd given up. Now, when I scream, "Dinner's ready!" she throws me my keys and goes and sits in the car. If it doesn't come in a box with a hermetically sealed action figure and ordered over a microphone, she's not eating. The other morning she tiptoed into my room and stuck her finger in my nose to see if I was awake.

"Mom, there's no milk for my cereal."

"Microwave the ice cream."

"But, it's, uh, Rocky Road."

Boy, is that ever saying a mouthful.

Kindergarten Kloset Kase

Every year it was a leap of faith whether we'd make it through the first month of school without family electroshock therapy. Our morning drill consisted of spilled milk, burnt toast, unmatched socks and a coin toss over whether to pour a cup of coffee...or a cup of Prozac.

When we finally sent our youngest child off to kindergarten, it compounded the confusion of getting her older brother and sister off to school with brown bag lunches that reeked of week-old tunafish and Funyuns; their homework that the printer, not the dog, ate; and $13.97, mostly in pennies, some pesos—that I vacuumed from in between the sofa cushions— for their field trip...to Federal Prison.

But even all the confusion didn't lessen the bells of freedom clanging in my ears. Since the second my OB told me to stop pushing, I had longed for the day all three kids would be in school. I dreamed of being in an empty nest that stayed picked up for 6 consecutive hours—all the toilet seats down, just me and the remote control, admiring my own private collection of dust.

But, oh, the angst we endured preparing our first child for her first day of kindergarten. After agonizing since her conception over which school was the ONLY school, that summer was focused on spelling bees, off-balance sheet accounting and shoe-tying contests, each with cash prizes. By her first day of K-garten, she could have read War and Peace upside down while tying double-knotted bows in her designer corrective shoes.

When it came time the following year for our son to head to kindergarten, we'd relaxed a little. After all, he'd learned everything he needed to know from Vanna White. The alphabet of course, (consonants only, go figure), but he also learned his numbers by counting her costume changes. I was reasonably confident that, between Velcro and Super Glue, he might even hold together until the 3:00 bell.

Maybe someday, I prayed, he'd make enough money to buy a vowel.

Then, along came our third child. Everything she needed to know, she learned from the third seat of the car. She answered all of her own questions, considered dog hair a condiment and, for her, happiness was not being left behind at the gas station.

As her senior citizen parents, we picked her school based on the timing of traffic lights and the number of handicapped parking spaces.

But, oh my, as chill as we were, what little we knew.

The night before school was to start, she looked at her dad sitting at the end of the dinner table, her eyes brimming with tears. Between quivering lips, she gulped, "Daddy, I don't know how to read."

"SURE you do," said her dad. "I taught all you kids how to read when you were three years old. Don't you remember that book I used to read to you every night?"

Her teenage werewolf brother said, "That was the VCR manual, dawg."

"No matter," he said, "there's no trick to reading. Just sound it out. What makes the sssss sound?"

"The VCR?" my daughter mumbled.

Her Valley Girl sister said, "If you, like, start now, Dad, she might, like, be able to read in time for her eye exam for her driver's license."

And then—exploding from our baby's lips, with one deep breath, she let it rip: "What if I can't find the bathroom? What if the teacher asks me my name and I throw up? What if the school catches on fire and I trip over my shoes because you never taught me how to tie them?

What if I spill my milk in the caft-e-ria...will the teacher yell at me as loud as you do?"

"No one yells louder than mom," her siblings chimed in chorus.

Then, with her last molecule of air, she squeaked, "What if I don't make any friends?"

Here I had been so consumed with teenage issues—body piercings, designated drivers and how to post bond—that I had failed a kid who knew this all-day school thing was big—more like HUGE.

For the next few weeks, I gave her chocolate cake for breakfast (don't you love parents who send their kids to school on a sugar high?) and drove her to school, reminding her to breathe, to take it one day at a time...and that we were there for her. (Well, her dad and I were—not so sure about her older brother and sister.) Each day as I walked her to her classroom, her hands were a little less sweaty...and her grip around my leg gradually loosened. And each day, her teacher welcomed her with a loving smile, knowing look and open arms.

Then one day, that baby bounced out of the car solo...and never looked back...except to say, "Stay put, mom. Your good-byes get kinda ugly."

Back home, amidst peace, quiet and dust, I contemplated my next life as a bail bondsman—until it was time to pick her up—and I listened as she told me how awesome her teacher was.

That's What Heroes Do

My eight-year-old just had her first date. What can I say?

She's the third child, the baby, the denouement, the tail wagging the dog. Rules for raising this child are different from our first couple of go-rounds—there aren't any. At least, we can't remember any. Our older kids beat them out of us.

She got her first credit card when she was five, drove a car at six and has applied for a discount pass for R-rated movies. She's never gone to bed before midnight or heard of vegetables or made up her bed. And now, in the second grade, she's dated a man old enough to be her father.

Fortunately, it *was* her father.

It had to be. Their date was to the Father-Daughter Lower School Dance.

"Dad, you can't be serious," rebuked our 14-year-old man of the world. "*'Real'* men," he explained, "don't dance." Spoken like a real man who doesn't know how.

As the official date, ol' dad knelt on the floor to pin on

his daughter's corsage—and stayed there. It wasn't his creaky bones or his bad back or even his blown-out knees that laid him out. It was shock—his "baby" looked anything but. As I watched my husband offer his arm to this younger woman, open her car door and speed away, I waved goodbye.

I could barely see.

The invitation to the dance was clear: No Moms Allowed. Which meant, of course, I had to get there quickly, before all the other uninvited, pushy, snooping mothers took the best peepholes.

The scene inside the dance looked like a lab experiment on hyperactivity. The place rocked—literally. Walls vibrated, dads' temples throbbed and Shirley Temple curls pulsated—frenetic energy fueled by double sugar cookies, Hawaiian punch and too much bass.

Pint-sized girls, dressed in killer tulle with feather boas and kiwi-colored toes poking out of platform shoes, scurried about. Gummed together in clumps of curls, they stuck out their tongues in a Whose-Is-Stained-by-the-Punch-Reddest competition, as they reeled in fits of laughter.

It was a sea of old men doubled over attempting to dance cheek-to-cheek with partners half their size, one-fiftieth their age with ninety-nine times the adrenaline. Given the age difference, it could've passed as a Junior Ms. Trophy Wife pageant.

For three hours, there was not one wallflower in the crowd as they danced to the classics: the "Chicken Dance", "Macarena", "Y.M.C.A.", and the "Ttwist", aging the dear old daddies an average of 23.7 years. Fortunately, the party package included a team of cardiologists and trauma experts with a crash cart.

In his eyes, she was the perfect date: she looked up to him, didn't try to lead and wanted to get home before the last rerun on *Nick at Nite*.

Once home at the end of a long evening, all she wanted was for him to tuck her into bed. He thanked heaven for little girls—as a veteran dad, he knows what lurks ahead in the teenage years: his IQ will plummet lower than his shoe size. He'll face the training bra, the driver's test, the prom and living in Heartbreak Hotel when she sends him on that familiar journey to the end of his rope.

For a dad, it is a trip worth taking…assuming that if he's done his job, she'll return to being his little girl when she grows up.

Without realizing, he had raised the bar, ruined the curve and set the standard for an future heartthrob who dares to enter her life.

As her dad, he believed he was the only man who'd ever be good enough for her. Yet, still, he wanted to be better. For her.

He held his breath…as well as the memory. It was some enchanted evening. She hugged the man she knew would give her the moon if she asked…because that's what heroes do.

Before drifting off to sleep, she whispered in his ear, "Next time, I think I'll lead."

And so the familiar journey begins.

Hello Muddah, Hello Faddah

All the counselors hate the waiters, and the lake has alligators, and The head coach wants no sissies, so he reads to us from Ulysses. *Now I don't want this should scare ya, but my bunkmate has malaria. You remember Jeffrey Hardy, They're about to organize a search party.*

—*Lyrics from "Camp Granada" song*

For that brief window in time when families across America pack the kids off to summer camp, there is pure joy in Mudville. The freedom! Staying up late and sleeping in, raiding the kitchen at 2 a.m., no carpools, no relatives, and, glory-be-to-God, no lectures.

If only the kids had it so good.

Unfortunately, from the moment a kid steps on the bus, his mother worries. It's her job.

Did the bus break down? Will they change their under-wear? Use Swim Ear? What if one of the 3,000 iron-on nametags falls off?

Not me. After nine months of living with two fire-breathing blocks of concrete who sit transfixed in front of the TV, a death grip on the remote control, refusing to acknowledge my presence, I care about only one thing: *Will they write?*

They can shout in letters and I won't hear them. They can complain about the counselor who yelled at them, their infected toe and the bad food...and I gloss over it. They can write about how they'll never send *their* kids away to some hole-in-the-wall filled with bugs, strangers and NO CABLE, for crying out loud. Yet, by the time I get the letter—because I happened to pack them off with last year's postage stamps— camp's almost over.

It's the perfect form of communication.

When our son was 10, he sent epistles of guilt:

Dear Mr. & Mrs. Parsley,

So far, camp is OK. Except I threw up. My counselor "Pyro" Pete said it was attitude sickness. But I might live. He smells weird—must be the Off! He sprays on his dreadlocks. The letters are smudged cause I just fished this out of the latrine. Everyone in my cabin cusses so much. I've learned a lot in one morning.

P.S. Send me some matches. Pyro says he may not have enough.

At age eight, our daughter chose her camp based on two things: distance and length, as in light years and months/away. She considered a space shuttle, but their tour of 12 weeks wasn't long enough. From her covered wagon in the Himalayas, she sent one postcard:

> Yo Ma 'n Pa!-How R U? Wuz up? Las' nite a bear came in our cabin...kool! Went hang-gliding n' one of my wings snapped right in 2...awsum! Two girls have boyfriends; two have girl friends. I hit 3 bull's-eyes in riflery! My tribe color is fewsha. Luv ya!
>
> P.S. Send some pics of my bro. Use'm as rifel targets.
>
> P.P.S. They said that next yeer, u shud probly pack sheets.

We never heard from her again.

Ahh, the power of communication. The things you learn—such as not to totally discount the space shuttle for next year, that English is her second language, and we really need a family gun control policy.

Meanwhile, Mr. Guilt Trip....

HELLOOOO! Is anybody there?
My best friend was Kyle, but he got food poisoning. Now it's Jose. They found a dead rat in the dishwasher and haven't washed dishes in 2 weeks. There's spaghetti sauce in the pears and gravy in the ice cream. I won the eyebrow-raising and tobacco-spitting contests. "Pyro" showed us how to make a blowtorch with a spray can of Lysol and a cigarette lighter. He said mine was the best. He should know. My other two counselors are co-dependent. One has the worst accent, like he's part Scottish-part Elvis. He's from Beaumont. He's a real @#%*.

No wonder the art of letter writing died. Too much information killed the reader.

Soon, they'll be home: fire-breathing concrete blocks that refuse to communicate with their mother.

I can hardly wait for school to start.

Wait a minute, it stopped hailing. Guys are swimming, guys are sailing.

Gee that's bettah. Muddah, Faddah kindly disregard this letter.

Wrinkle in the Road

Car trips have been as central to this family's summer nervous system as Bob Hope was to "Road to" movies. There's just something so American about crossing the country in an oversized vehicle with an under-sized carburetor crammed with five bodies holding pea-sized bladders, two dogs who sweat through their tongues and Tom Jones wailing on an eight-track tape.

What most families called "wholesome togetherness," I called masochism—the older kids' drawing lines in permanent marker down the youngest child, stuffing handfuls of Cheerios into the a.c. vents and spitting 1,327 sesame seeds out of the window—while it's rolled up. Try communicating with someone who never took off his headphones; or one who, drugged with Dramamine, drooled all the way to California; or one who pouted for 800 miles after her brother tossed her Barney video out the window somewhere near Amarillo.

Like the tortoise and the hare, The Bob and I had slightly

different approaches to car trips. When I get behind the wheel, it's a race—against time, against other cars, against all odds that we'll arrive safely. Pit stops are for sissies. What is meant to be a relaxing time during a leisurely tour of the country turns into a marathon of blurred horizons as we streak across state after state. They complain that seeing the geyser Old Faithful in the dark and shining our headlights on natural phenomena like Mt. Rushmore just doesn't do it for them.

My husband, on the other hand, will stop anywhere they sell T-shirts, pork rinds and Mountain Dew. "They're quick energy," he says between bites. Wiping his mouth on the sleeve of his "Baby on Board" T-shirt, he lectures on the value of good nutrition, waving a Twinkie in the air for punctuation.

Feeling like the lesser half of a team of explorers, I point out to The Bob that perhaps we should've taken a left in Oklahoma three days earlier. But I know from experience that I'd have more success conducting world peace talks than convincing Meriwether to stop for directions. At least Lewis and Clark made it back home...even if it was over two years later.

Other than a toothbrush, I have nothing in common with these people. I can't talk to The Bob without hurling four-letter words, "WEST—go West!" And I have no interest in trying to explain to my kids, who think the Reagan era was when *The Exorcist* was released, what life was like before answering machines, microwaves or MTV. Of course, in their eyes I'm so old they think I went through puberty with the Andrews Sisters and handed the pen to Lincoln to sign the Emancipation Proclamation.

So I look older than I am, which is not as old as they think, and act the age I wish I looked, but don't want to be.

Oh, Lord, I am starting to think like them.

By the time they are old enough to have a civilized conversation with me, sharing their innermost secrets, I'll probably be too old to remember the details...or their names. Or care. On our next trip, they'll probably chip in and give me dog tags and an electronic anklet so I'll know who I am, and they'll know where. I'll pay for the trip to Disney World *and* be the one in the stroller.

Nothing to say, I stare out the window. One eye on the side view mirror, I keep my mind's eye on the future—through the bug-splattered windshield, beyond the days when the kids won't go to the corner store for fear of being seen with me, across the years when they are too consumed with college/work/life to travel with us. And when they are on the other side of life...planning car trips with their own kids.

In the backseat of their lives will sit a much older version of me, humming "Green Green Grass of Home", asking every thirty seconds, "Are we there, yet?"

Gobble, Gobble

The turkey is breathing down my neck. Thanksgiving is days away and all I've done is hose down the dining room, nail down the furniture and highlight my stash of take-out menus. Soon, 137 people, some of whom I actually may know, will invade to break my bread, bank account and Queen Anne chairs. I've counted the good plastic plates, forks and glasses three times and, if they eat in shifts, I can serve seven—with stained chopsticks, 23½.

But there's more missing than a few place settings. Somewhere along the line in the fast-food joints, I forgot to teach my human-gobblers table manners. They eat with their chins perched on the table, shovel forkfuls (if only they had a fork) into mouths that never completely close, and pass food by bending back a spoon full of mashed potatoes that's spring-loaded with a rubber band yelling, "Thar she blows!" Forget enlightening dinner conversation. They're too busy burping the alphabet. With their napkins folded in a triangle and tied around their heads, one corner sticking straight up, they look like a round-table of bishops voting on a new pope.

How did this happen? I had good manners once. "Please" and "thank you" were required if we wished to continue breathing on our own. Elbows on the table were stabbed with a serving fork, napkins were stapled to our chins, *and* we did the dishes. Try that today and kids will sue.

But I must admit, there was something about my own extended family gatherings and the arrival of my cousins that brought out more than just a little of the Wild Turkey in all of us.

Our holiday ritual started each year with the princess who threw a hissy fit, holding her breath until she was allowed to wear her Christmas dress, tiara and white tasseled go-go boots. As if it mattered—her brother was still in his Halloween costume. There was the couple no one recognized who insisted their child-prodigy play "Tie a Yellow Ribbon" on his harmonica, while his evil twin banged her head on the piano. It wasn't long before someone dipped the harmonica in Tabasco and Crazy Glued the piano keys.

When dinner was served, the "little" table had all the action. Each year, we'd pile all the vegetables into the iced tea pitcher, except for the two peas in Tommy's nose, along with a cup of pepper, Sweeta and chocolate syrup. Then we'd draw straws, except for the two stuck in Tommy's ears, to see who had to drink it—and we'd all double-dog swear to pool our pocket change and help pay for the kid's brain transplant. There was Cousin Joey who was always escaping from the table to lock himself in the bathroom, trying to figure out where the water goes after he yanked the handle. One year he brought goggles, flippers and a depth charge. His mother claimed he was adopted, but when he wiped his mouth with his shirt collar, we knew he was blood.

The year we got a Lazy Susan, we invited the entire convent next door to dinner. My brother gave it one good heave-ho and the ketchup, mustard and cranberry sauce splattered across Sister Celia's habit. Had Sister been wearing a canvas, she'd be hanging at the MoMA.

Now that we're grown, it's the big table from which all blessings flow. Uncle Otto's always borrowing Uncle Edgar's keys to his Volvo—to clean his ears. There's so much wax buildup that, with a wick and a match, those keys could burn until Easter. There's the great-aunt's fifth husband who sells used trailer homes and has three toupees. We wager on which one he'll wear: 1) just had a haircut; 2) need a haircut or 3) gelled.

As ruler of the roost, my husband carves the turkey and blesses the food—most of which is shoveled down in the buffet line. He's a guy—the only meat he really wants to see carved is under a helmet. For 13,577 first downs over four days, he'll watch overgrown men in tight pants on TV try to maim each other, forcing vital organs out of their bodies—a scene eerily similar to the one around his own dinner table. "In the name of Favre, the Center and the Holy Sport, Hail Mary!"

Who cares about place settings in a house that's etiquette-free? What's Thanksgiving without watching feathers fly and my flock of gobblers gobble? It's tradition.

By nightfall, I'm ready to escape the maddening crowd, eat leftovers alone in the closet and try to imagine life without these people. Except I can't.

Family sees us at our best and our worst...and keeps the faith that the best shall prevail. They teach us how to laugh, how to cry, how to fight and how to forgive. They scold us, nurture us, humble us, teach us patience and right from wrong. They challenge us to make the world a better place, then set us free...sort of. No matter how long we stay away, they save a place for us. In times of joy, they're the people with whom we want to celebrate. And in times of adversity, the ones we lean on for support.

Even if they are all such turkeys that I expect their thermometers to popup any minute.

But I suppose I do find some solace knowing that my young turks haven't fallen far from the tree. After all, I'm the Queen of Turkey, looking pretty dad-gum regal in my new Christmas dress, tiara and white tasseled go-go boots.

Miss Manners, eat your heart out.

The Birds and the Beers

I knew I'd blow it.

Standing in the checkout line at the grocery store, I fell into one of the great pitfalls of parenthood. My six-year-old angel who'd waited, I guess, all her life, asked above the din, "WHERE DO BABIES COME FROM?!"

The sacker sank, the checker checked out and the Muzak was muted, all were waiting for my answer. I felt like E. F. Hutton about to read the Kinsey Report.

Certainly when I was her age, I never asked my mother that question. I knew where babies came from—the hospital. That was until the fifth grade when I saw "the film." Like hogs to slaughter, the girls were led into the library. Lying in wait, to our surprise, were our mothers standing silently in the back of the room. The very back. In the dark. With paper bags over their heads.

"The film" was intended to facilitate "the talk" between moms and daughters. Ours consisted of three little words.

"Any questions?" she asked, her hands shaking.

"No," I croaked.

Any other answer could have led to discussing *things*—of which I was certain mothers knew nothing. Nor should they. And I sure-as-shootin' wasn't going to be the one to tell *my* mother.

At age 15, I got the full story, taught in vivid detail, the way it's been taught for years. In the high school bathroom... by the girls who smoked.

Over in the boys' bathroom, "experts"—defined as guys with the tallest stacks of *Playboy*—held complete seminars. "Experts" typically had cricks in their necks from holding the centerfolds sideways under their covers at night with a flashlight under their chin. Who needed biology? They got the drift.

As a young mother, I decided to be "open," tackling this delicate issue with my kids while they were young— preferably before they could talk. There'd be fewer questions. And I knew that when they were older—say, six—they'd feel comfortable coming to me to discuss "it."

Unfortunately, they felt more comfortable discussing "it" with the big kid down the street. He was 7. He'd learned every-thing he needed to know from his older brother. He was 9. I'd never met the older brother personally, but I'll bet he was the kid whose neck was so crooked he looked like he was riding his bike backwards.

The boys made a blood pact: they'd pray for X-ray vision. And not because they wanted to be radiologists. They wanted to see London. They wanted to see France. They wanted to see someone's Frederick's of Hollywood anything.

When I sat my son down as a pre-teen to discuss *life*, I got as far as "The birds..."

He interrupted, "Save your breath. Saw the movie. Loved the part when the whole town got pecked to death." But later, watching the national news together and President Clinton's contribution to the blue dress, what was left to talk about—other than his aspiration to become President?

For high school biology, he wrote a research paper on reproduction. Proofing it, I understood almost none of it—until page 239. When he realized that certain somethings rang a bell with me, he made me promise that, as a biological mother of three, I had no—nor ever intended to have—first-hand knowledge of such *things*. I promised.

Open, honest communication—particularly lying—is key when raising well-adjusted, sex-crazed citizens.

Since then, I've encountered another pitfall of parent-hood—when the kids reach the legal drinking age, which most swear is 12. Once again, I exposed my kids early.

In a case of mistaken identity, I accidentally gave my first baby a bottle of apple juice. Well, I thought it was apple juice. Sure looked like apple juice. Actually, it was scotch. Single malt. A gag gift—scotch in a baby bottle—that my mother-in-law had sent to me in the hospital since the one thing we agreed upon was our love of the same brand.

My baby sucked it down. Had that happened today, I'd be writing from jail. She was the only 14-month-old that could do cartwheels across the pediatrician's office. In Mother's Day Out, other kids counted 1-2-3. She recited the entire twelve-step program.

So when my youngest asked me in the checkout line at the grocery store, "Where do babies come from?" I thought about open, honest communication—and stated with convic-tion, "A bottle of wine and a James Taylor album."

I blew it. I knew I would.

Father, Son and Holy Coach

In the Big-Inning, God created Little League. And it was good. So good, in fact, it became an organized religion. Which is why, each spring, entire families get on their knees to pray to the lords of Little League. Kids pray for a strong arm. Dads pray someone else will coach. I pray for a bumper crop of nachos, beef jerky and Sour Powers so I don't have to cook until after Williamsport.

Legions of green pea Babe-Ruth-wannabes fill the fields. Managers fill unemployment lines—their newly gained status after leaving work at 2:30 four times a week for practice. Parents look to Coach to set an example; to treat the kids, umpires and other coaches with respect, calling them "Bonehead" only behind their backs; and to identify a kid's raw talent. "Talent" in this case is defined as a mom with a Victoria's Secret model's body and a pool for team parties.

When my husband coached, he was totally laid-back... during pre-season. At the team meeting, everyone agreed with Coach. "We'll have fun. It's just a game, for crying out loud."

"Crying out loud" being the operative phrase.

At the first game, some dads threw gloves...with kids' arms still attached, shook clenched fists and yelled, "Maim, kill, win! Think college! Think ESPY!" There's a baseball term for this syndrome, I believe: E.R.A.—Egos Run Amuck.

Our team, which faced many forks in the road, took all of them. Remembering second base came after first was a challenge. The right-, no, left-, no, right-handed pitcher. The girl—a girl—who threw harder than her dad, but cried when her nail polish chipped. Questions hollered from the dugout, "Mom, if I hit the ball this season, how 'bout Disney World?" were overshadowed only slightly by questions in the field, "How many fingers am I holding up?"

But, oh, the pride we felt when our son caught his first

pop fly. Even if it was his cup that had flown out from inside his pants.

Mid-season, we were 0-7. Looking like Tommy Lasorda on steroids, Coach had a bleeding ulcer, shingles and had lost clumps of hair. Two losses later, our son played third base with a bag over his head. When the season ended 0-15, Coach had split into so many personalities, he could've had a family reunion with himselves. We threatened that his next outing would be an exorcism if he ever coached again. But he re-upped anyway. "We'll have fun," he said—just before we shot him.

Every day for ten years, I watched my son outside the kitchen window throw 390,345 pitches into a net, diving to catch each one, his glove the size of a Volvo. Even an idiot mom respects passion like that. Baseball was his dad's first love. Now it's his.

He loved it for the dirt and the spitting and the sleeping in his uniform. He loved it for its endless possibilities—blasting 101 homers over the fence, beating the tag and sliding into home...if only in his imagination. He loved it for the stories, reliving every play from Tadpoles through Seniors with his pals and his dad. He loved it for the sheer guyness: that moms were there only to get ice packs, find the birth certificate and cheer...silently. He loved it because when he was playing, it marked a time when all that mattered was the game.

Even now, separated by miles of both distance and time from the glory days, these boys of summer still share that love.

"Dad, remember in Minors when I hit the fence and you yelled, 'Foul, foul!' and I slumped back home, picked up my bat as the ump said, 'What are you doing?'"

... and it was good.

Vim...and Vinegar

Each year, the end of school feels like the burning of Atlanta. Kids torch the neighborhood, preparing their Science Fair project...then there's Reconstruction.

Entering my daughter's Science Fair this year, I wore the usual Hazmat suit—what I forgot was a cocktail shaker and my bartender's guide. *Does salt help H2O conduct electricity?* The tequila is harmless, it's the ice in a margarita that curls your hair. *Does temperature affect the life span of bubbles?* Hot beer lasts longer, but...who cares?

What some called "experiments" are daily rituals in my home. *Does sight affect taste?* You betcha—napkins make great blindfolds. *How long does it take bread to grow mold?* Eight weeks—then it's liquid. *How do you make glue from milk?* Wait eight weeks, plus one day.

And my favorite: *How to Launder Money.* Talk about a bright future. But there, in the fine print: soak old pennies in vinegar.

It's not just the Science Fair. There's Save Tibet Week, Left-handers for the Metric System, and Duct Tape Awareness, all requiring costumes.

In pre-K, my son had to be a blowfish for Deep "Thee" Week—Flipper goes Shakespeare. I slapped some red lipstick on him and his sister's tutu, stuffed his cheeks with Brussels sprouts, and chased him across the carpet in his socks until his hair stood on end. If it'd been Cross-Dresser Week, we'd be talking blue ribbon.

In the sixth grade, my daughter landed the lead role in the school play. Fairy princess? Rock star? "Accused murderer," she said flatly. "I need a costume." If she pled temporary insanity, I had an entire wardrobe that would send her to the gas chamber. The next year, she was cast as a dangling participle. I told her she was on her own.

Fortunately, I've lived long enough to get past the humiliation of competing with Wonder-Mothers, the ones who can turn a collection of navel lint, lace doilies and an old tablecloth into Martha Washington's inaugural ball gown. But it's cost me. For the Medieval festival, I rented our daughter's costume: gold brocade, period shoes, real-hair wig...and a lawyer to read the contract.

But she paled compared to others. One boy wore a gold chasuble and white damask silk mitre. "I'm Pope Urban II," he said proudly. "Why Pope Urban II?" I asked. "Because there was already a Pope Urban I." Ba-da-bum.

St. Bridget explained to me that after 8 children, she became a nun. Slow learner...it only took me three. Richard the Lion-Hearted proudly announced he'd led the Third Crusade—but wearing his grandmother's antique brooch? And the poor mother of overscheduled Machiavelli, Mr. "End-Justifies-the-Means." He marched on Pisa...in his Little League uniform and cleats.

When I was in second grade, I did what every kid did for Fire Prevention Week—got my dad to do it. Like Edward Scissorhands, he deftly cut up my mom's favorite blouse, his VW Bug manual and the caned seats of our breakfast room chairs...to weave a laundry basket, of course. Flipping through his English-German dictionary, he was done. His fire prevention tip?

NEVER PARK YOUR VOLKSWAGEN
NEAR YOUR WASSERHEISENTUNK

Embarrassed? Thought I'd be the first kid to be burned at the stake celebrating Fire Prevention. No one knew what it meant, but they sure never parked their car between a laundry basket and a hot water heater.

At this point in the school year, one parent I know would gladly pay $1,000 to avoid school projects.

Imagine how much that will save me in vinegar?

In the In-between

There is a brief moment...

after the anniversary candles set fire to the new drapes; stiletto heels have pockmarked the linoleum floor; and the champagne cork misfires, cracking the 90-gallon glass aquarium...

after the kindergarten graduation when nephews have flattened the pansies rollerblading; spiked the iced tea with Tabasco; and thinned gunky mud pies with hundred-year-old scotch...

after the Christmas presents have been opened and angelic nieces have tied their cousin's sash to the ceiling fan; their great-aunt's orthopedic shoelaces together; and made Play-Doh with someone's $60 moisturizer and $50 camouflage face powder...

after the wake when the sister-in-law rolls her eyes as she spots the fishnet Leg Lamp she thought she should've inherited, the cracked leatherette sofa and faux fur pillows, and the R-rated photos in the powder room...

after the Thanksgiving turkey's wishbone has been snapped, the kids have used someone's silk tie to leash the dog to the andirons; flooded the upstairs closet; and played keep-away with the last of their great-great-grandmother's porcelain figurines...

after the hand mixer has replastered the walls with birthday cake batter, the class hamster has given birth in the kitty litter, and the pet snake is announced missing...

after the ooh and ahhs over the baby shower presents, the cat sharpens his claws in the silver closet; the blender explodes; and the next-door neighbor is pickled...

after the retirement dinner when too many cooks have torched the kitchen; the Cornish hen's pop-up timer has melted; and the last fireman leaves...

after the chair is pulled out from under the Maid of Honor; the antique linen napkins have mopped up the spilled Bloody Marys...and dad, raising his glass to toast his new son-in-law, chips the last fine crystal goblet with his fork...

But...

before the toddler swigs the last drops from the "empty" beer cans; the dog hacks up the chicken bone on the Oriental rug; and the first trip to the E.R...

before the top to the salt shaker falls into the soup; the ladle sinks into the gravy; and the first fistful of sweet potatoes flies across the children's table...

before grandma's snores make the chair slats rattle; the uncle goes into anaphylactic shock mistaking shrimp for a pig-in-a-blanket; and you hide in the closet writing your own ransom note...

before talk turns to religion, politics and plastic surgery; the disposal chews up the silverware; and you think the Osbourne family has nothing over you...

before the first kickoff; the first first down; and the first fist-fight over a ref's call...

before the cigars fire up, the turkey's tryptophan kicks in, and the case of port you hid for that special occasion is drained...

Just before the same old stories are embellished. Lines drawn and credit taken, it happens—after the before; before the after—the in-between.

The moment when arms extend and hands are offered around the table. When thoughts calm, breaths soften, and noise and confusion are suspended.

There, in a brief respite of peace, fingers delicately lace together, intertwining life cycles and open hearts. There, in the stillness, in the twinkling of serenity, silent things on the other side of the everyday world can be heard. Rising above, carried by a swirl of events generations-old, is a glorious exception—seen and felt with perfect crispness.

Life's ordinary miracles.

Family gatherings. Ticking off milestone events. Our stories. As individual as puzzle pieces fitting together to illustrate the larger picture of who we are and why we're here. Bite-size pieces of life, purpose, hope, and gratitude. Tiny sprigs of appreciation for the ones around us. The ones who make us, us...each one a part of everyone else.

Blessings in disguise only take a moment to savor—and a lifetime to forget.

A Patch of Parsley

They said we'd never last. Me, who revels in time alone, marrying The Bob, the oldest of ten, the Captain of his own family football team. The patriarch who defines "alone" as... well, how would he know?

Two+ decades, nine spouses and 32 cousins later, we hosted his family reunion. "Hey," said the Captain, "not all of 'em can come." "Not all," numbering 33, headed for our two-bedroom house on the Guadalupe River in the Hill Country of Texas. "It's overdue." After all, we hadn't been together since Father's Day...five whole days earlier.

The forecast: thunderstorms. The Doppler radar: crimson. Charcoal skies looming, they paraded down our driveway, a seamless stream of bodies toting armfuls of Tostitos, Coffee-Mate and chardonnay—life's essentials.

Instantly, the kids fled for the wide, open yard as limitless, in their young eyes, as their imagination. Dodging thunder-clouds, days were consumed with pranks, double-dog-dares, calling "shotgun" on the favored spot on the overstuffed sofa, the favorite soft drink, the favorite inner tube to explore the far side of the river. And the river's rite of passage: lunging from a rope swing dangling from a high-bough tree, splashing, yards below, into the icy water. Boldly-striped beach towels dotted the porch rails, spelling in their own Morse code, "Life is good." After naps, wide-eyed and barefoot, play resumed with chocolate-covered mouths and elbows dripping in fresh peach juice.

Nights were reserved for the rodeo...sitting so close to the ring, you could wipe the sweat from the bull rider's brow; chasing tails in the calf scramble, shuffling across the dirt-n-dung in open-toed Tevas. And, later, the dance—23 kids doing their best version of the Two-Step, mouthing 1-2; 1-2-3—some counting as high as they could.

At last, the barbeque. So many aunts and uncles that confusion ruled. Small hands tugged on nameless pant legs, needing help toasting a marshmallow; young pyromaniacs begging to stoke their passion by adding one more wad of newspaper to the bonfire...asking unabashedly, "Hey, what's your name again?"

Sparklers in hand, kids danced like fireflies, spelling their names as jagged points of light punctured the dark night air. Unrestricted by the sun or the moon, unconscious of where family ends and friendships begin, they were completely present in the moment.

Used to my quirky, small-family ways, they no longer

noticed when I'd slip away. Away from the sleeping porch filled with little ones dreaming. Away from the teenager's house glowing from late-night movies. Away from the porches brimming with blissfully tired, off-duty parents.

Under the canopy of croaking cicadas, I listened to the rise and fall of gentle conversation and their laughter's rhythm. Sharing four decades together, these siblings have fought, forgiven, grieved, celebrated, separated, matured and peered inward, their reflection mirroring their parents. The only light illuminating the cloud-covered sky was theirs—the glow of connectedness.

For four days these hills were alive. Tears of laughter, interspersed with tears over splintered toes and stolen toys, hummed across our skin.

After the favorite uncle, whom they lovingly called Aunt Tom, fatally hit an innocent turtle on the highway, he was jokingly renamed Aunt T.K....Turtle Killer. After the not-so-favorite aunt Uncle Weezer grew hoarse from barking, "SHUT. THE. DOOR," I became known, not-so-lovingly, as Mrs. Weezer.

After all the sheets were washed, the towels folded; after all the doors were shut tightly—at last—the welcome mats caked in mud and the rugs decorated with brightly colored cookie crumbs, it was time to leave.

As the last car pulled away, the clouds, swollen and bruised, holding four days of rain, spilled forth. Buckets of enormous drops created rivulets, filling the paths once beaten by small feet.

Alone, silent memories filled the Hill Country air.

And they said we'd never last.

All in the State of Mind

Sitting outside the principal's office, I waited, beads of sweat forming on my brow. The last time I encountered a principal, I'd skipped classes in high school. Unfortunately, she did not believe me when I told her that, in my faith, Bruce Springsteen's birthday was a religious holiday.

Twenty years later: I mopped my brow as my firstborn tested for admission into first grade.

With two children on the ground and the third kicking to get out and get started, I filled out the application, wondering if I wrote "Rastafarian" next to "Religion," how many holidays would that guarantee?

My husband, the math whiz, doodled on his palm. "Guess what?" he shrieked. "When Elizabeth graduates from eighth grade, the baby will be starting kindergarten!"

"You could've gone all day without saying that," I spat. But he didn't understand my fear—and not just because I was talking through a barf bag.

Flash forward fifteen years: the baby who was kicking to get out is now kicking to get out of middle school. And, surreal as it is, her older sister is graduating from college.

This week will be my last carpool to this school that provided the educational foundation for my children. No more writing tardy notes because I overslept; submitting homework with teeth marks (mine, math); or delivering forgotten lunches containing PB & J sandwiches with the crust cut off. Pity— another few years and I just might have fallen in step with the after-school carpool system run with the warmth of the Third Reich.

I will say goodbye to the teachers who taught them how to sound out "supercalifragilisticexpealidocious," write with creative flair and use their toes to do the times table. I will hug the coaches who taught hopeful young athletes how to run the length of the field, foul without getting caught, and that hurdles in life continue beyond the track.

Success, they explained, is more than points on a scoreboard; it's a state of mind—if you think you can, you will.

With moist eyes, I will wave one last time to Officer Davis, the traffic cop who, with her sunny glow and cool-wave jazz moves, danced in the intersection and into the heart of every schoolchild. Angelic protector/matchmaker, Officer Davis taught her kids life's greatest lessons: always look both ways, hold hands, and stick together.

As I pack up the last vestiges of our middle school identity—the laminated carpool number; the faded, frayed collared shirts; bulletproof skirts with chiseled plaid pleats and gray socks whose holes exposed bare toes—I'll give thanks for this third time around.

Stressed out while cutting our teeth on our first two, we chilled enough to seize the opportunity to savor each moment with our youngest—she who lightened our steps, quickened our breaths and, with dancing eyes, restored noise to our home...be it the phone ringing or girls squealing. With graying hair and degenerating spines, we know too well that this, too, shall pass...all too quickly.

Through her, we soon will relive her sister's and brother's high school issues—designated drivers, unfair curfews and posting bond, knowing that in the time it takes a facial tic to become our only form of exercise, she'll be applying to college.

But thanks to life lessons learned during her lower and middle school years, when she goes out into the world, she, along with her siblings, will look both ways, hold hands, and stick together.

And know that success is all in the state of mind.

Magic in a House of Glass

To my mind's eye, they only come out when children are around—like fairies, pixie dust and Santa Claus. The lightning bugs are there, of course, every summer evening, but a child's eye brings them to life.

As dusk pulls down its nighttime shade over our Hill Country home, the delicate, glowing creatures hover like a layer of twinkling Christmas lights strung between the lush grass blanket and air inking to black.

When I first discovered them as a child, Aunt Louise pulled a Mason jar down from the shelf and punctured its metal lid with the dulled tip of my Great-Uncle Scott's ice pick. I ran to join the other kids visiting for the summer who were scavenging the yard, our parents watching from the porch of our cinder-block house. Gently, they'd transfer the blinking treasures from our small, softly cupped hands, and place our flashing yellow diamonds into their new house of glass.

We wanted to keep them forever, but, after tapping on the jar, trying to make them light on command, we'd tire over our lack of control and let them go. Then we would count the hours until the next night when we could do it all over again.

The mauve hours of our Hill Country mornings were consumed with business—releasing tiny florets of dandelions into the wind, stalking ants to incinerate, and counting dead armadillos along the river road. Roasting with impatience, sometimes we'd bring its leathery shell of armor inside the house and sling it over our heads. The things we'd do trying to speed up the adults who were wasting our time lazily filling picnic baskets to tote down to the river.

For the rest of the day, the rope swing swayed back and forth like a perfectly timed metronome, kids taking turns dangling off the end before dropping into the chilling water, vying for the World's Biggest Belly Flop. I romped through my days on the river, twirling and somersaulting in the water, a weightless, shining goddess with a zinc oxide-coated nose in a two-sizes-too-small pink swimsuit that rode up my backside, exposing more than it covered.

Our house, the color of lemons, was the stage for our summer stock. We produced Greek tragedies such as *Thoroughly Modern Millie* and *Sound of Music*. Magic shows, our renowned repertoire of tricks promising to make anyone who annoyed us disappear. Later, sitting in a puddle of lamplight under the fort of blankets spanning the ceiling fan, twin beds and window unit, we talked of our famous futures; how we'd live in a split-level home with shag carpet, a mirrored bar, and a kitchen stocked only with M&M's, candy cigarettes and Bosco.

Reality was for the unimaginative.

Deeper into the summer, when deer would debut their new, velvet antlers, we'd lay under the Full Buck Moon. We would trace shooting stars, look for signs of thunderstorms, and count the days until the goldenrods appeared, drawing the curtain on our lazy summer days.

The lightning bugs lit my way to maturity. But somewhere along that journey, I stopped seeing them. Perhaps life took on too many distractions. Perhaps I spent my days and nights providing the things one needs to survive and forgetting the things that make us smile.

When I had children, the lightning bugs returned. Maybe they were waiting for me to return, too. As I pulled down from the shelf the container of my childhood, I felt the magic return. Watching them cup their small hands around these creatures confirmed the value of holding things you love loosely...and learning to let them go.

Hundreds of seasons have cycled in our lives and, while my kids still enjoy baking on a float in the river and filling their lungs with the pureness of the night air, the lightning bugs no longer beckon them.

I wait for the day when the musculature of grace unfolds its arms welcoming them back to this place that will sustain them in their mauve hours...and, someday, share this with their own kids. I will draw down for them from the same shelf, the milky Mason jar with the rusty metal lid crudely punctured with the dulled tip of my Great-Uncle Scott's ice pick. And delight in watching the magic return once again...inside small, softly cupped hands.

The Chauffeur Years

My life and office behind-the-wheel, it became clear that while I initially delivered my kids in a hospital, my true calling was to deliver them to malls, tae kwon do/baton twirling/sword-swallowing lessons and $10,000 birthday parties across a city of 600 square miles...sometimes across the country...always during rush hour.

But drive them I did—to eavesdrop.

Given their natural tendency to burrow themselves behind closed bedroom doors, underneath headphones and inside the TV, the car was the only place I might get lucky enough to devour a morsel of information about their secret lives. Like a lioness stalking my prey, hungrily I vetted their one friend who had not only loose lips but also a certain cluelessness that anyone old enough to drive might not be deaf.

When the older two got their driver's licenses, one year apart, conversations evolved from the length of his hair, her skirt and my fuse to...insurance. The first time they backed out of our driveway, they hit their father's car. Then mine.

In a weak attempt to discuss matters of safety, I went from being tongue-tied as I touched on drugs, alcohol and the definition of sex to being speechless when one called home at midnight asking, "Uh, what's our deductible?"

Scared of all the monsters that lay in wait for them in the big world? You bet. Yet, I didn't know fear until I heard the news of a school shooting or car accident, holding my breath until I heard their voices. When they didn't call at the appointed hour—or second—or missed their curfew by two minutes, I would lunge at them upon sight, the mix of love and fear having catapulted me into imagining the worst-case scenario. As my husband lay snoring.

Traversing their childhood to adolescence, my fervent prayer morphed from "Keep them on time" to "Keep them safe."

But if ever there was a constant, spanning the bridge from my holding on to their innocence to living my life as a chauffeur, it was…Capital "G" Guilt.

If only I'd read *Goodnight Moon* one more time, listened to their prayers longer, believed her when she said her arm was broken or he said he'd swallowed a jack. If only I hadn't gone into labor before my final Lamaze class. Maybe then I would've been a good mother.

Like many things in life, I may not have known how to do it the right way, but I knew how not to do it—and that was to be one of those pushy mothers. The kind who made excuses, blaming outside forces for their children not making the All-Star team, being robbed of a blue ribbon or were two/tenths of a point shy of making Honors Algebra.

Yet, without realizing, I'd become just that. Instead of listening to the labor nurse when she told me to stop pushing, I'd just begun. Pushing them to think outside the box, be their own person, find their passion. Make a difference.

I continued to make more predictions about their futures

than a two-bit psychic.

Our oldest, quiet and reserved, I just knew, was destined to be a CEO. Until a small reading problem was detected when she had difficulty spelling CEO.

Ever-armed with toy guns, a look that would melt steel and a brain spewing baseball stats—a kid who wouldn't go to a drive-thru because he'd be away from home too long—I pegged my son as either a hired gun or a Bat Boy who would live in our garage.

The baby, of course, would always be the baby, the one who would love us into our drooling years.

My Lord, I thought I was smart.

Driving Ms. Crazy

I had a nightmare the other night. I was flying through a jungle on a roller coaster at the speed of light, tree branches swiping my face, my cheeks slapping me senseless in gale-force winds. Wild animals the size of 18-wheelers lunged in front of me, forcing the car to careen off-course, popping my head back and forth like a yo-yo. I frantically stamped my right foot on the floorboard hoping to hit a brake, but there was nothing there. Slowly, the blurred image of a steering wheel came into focus on my left. Sitting behind it, drenched in sweat, was my 15-year-old kid. This was no dream...

My daughter is a "Student Driver."

There is no preparation for this moment. One day, the little angel is strapped in her infant seat, practicing projectile vomiting; the next, smushing Twinkies between the car seats, screaming that her bratty brother crossed the line onto *her* side of the back seat. Then suddenly, practically without warning, the state declares her old enough to navigate a machine the size of the Titanic.

When God created teenagers, He was pretty up front that, sure, the world will probably come to an end...but first, there would be Driver's Ed. As if that isn't chilling enough, the learner's-permit-age happens to hit about the sametime a girl's body is under siege by raging hormones. If we survive this stage, we can still look forward to the end of the world.

Compounding the problem is my daughter's need to prove that she is in complete control, which, in her mind, is best achieved by cranking all of the control knobs on the car stereo to TILT. This way, unsuspecting motorists are put on notice that she is in the vicinity. When the hood of their car, their chest wall and cranial lining begin vibrating to the classic beat of Eminem or Snoop Dog, other drivers will know that she could be as close as two blocks away.

I used to love the car. It was my favorite place to hide. From under the third seat, I could complete a thought, calm my eye twitch and steady my trembling hands long enough to take my pills. The little ones who used to drive me under the third seat are now driving me around the corner, around town, and, ultimately, around the bend.

Of course, my daughter would prefer that a blow-up doll ride shotgun, but until she gets her real license at 16, she needs her old lady. Preferably, her insurance card. With insurance, the hospital is more likely to treat an unsuspecting motorist who gets in the way as my daughter cruises down the runway of life.

My husband views having a new driver in the family as an opportunity to bond with his teenager, listen to her thoughts and dreams, discuss world events and talk batting averages. The first time he rode shotgun, she crept along so slowly that by the time they returned home, the old man was eligible for AARP.

When I had my first "go," I lost my sense of feeling and ability to speak by the time we pulled out of the driveway. I learned to carry a legal pad to communicate: "You're driving a lethal weapon!" "Using your windshield wipers does not indicate a left turn." "Don't pick your teeth in the rear-view mirror when you're entering the freeway!" "A yellow light does not mean *floor* it!"

We never got around to talking about what she wanted to be when she grew up because, well, nothing is a given.

Just the other day while we were screaming down the Interstate, I saw something that made me feel better. In the lane next to us was a white-paneled eighteen-wheeler with gigantic red letters across the back:

CAREFUL—STUDENT DRIVER

As we zipped past the truck in a blur, I'm pretty certain that I saw what was probably the driver's old lady riding shotgun. She appeared to be fumbling through her purse.
No doubt looking for her insurance card.

Car Wars

As most guys approach middle age—sometime around their 15th birthday—they begin to question what is really important in life. *Have I made my first million? Have I conquered my feminine side? Can I belch the entire National Anthem?* But until they give in to their innermost, uncontrollable desire for...for...OCTANE does the meaning of life become clear: Cars.

The obsession begins brewing on the playground where small boys growl and sputter *vroom* as they mow down their friends, leaving Hot Wheels tire tracks down their backs, over their hands and through their hair. Then, as if without warning—*crash!*—they really are behind the wheel, and it's time to rename your driveway Dead Man's Curve.

I thought I was prepared. I'd just survived driver's ed a year ago with my daughter, thanks to a pacemaker and fistfuls of Valium. I didn't know how good I had it. To her, the chief purpose of the hood was to hold the ornament. My son prefers to think of it as a crash pad for pedestrians.

"I'm in a *Suburban* for cryin' out loud!" he yells. "Don't these people know I have the right-of-way?" I respond calmly, with my hands around his throat, "Not. when. you. are. DRIVING. ON. THE. JOGGING. TRAIL!"

Whenever he sees a girl, he slows down, tosses me a paper bag and hisses, "Put this on and act like a crash dummy." I told him I don't need the bag. Riding with him, I know what it feels like to be a bull careening through the streets of Pamplona.

After a few more drive-bys, I started wearing a hard hat—in my kitchen. The garage wall is neither dense enough nor obvious enough to make him come to a full stop. I expect him to crash through at any moment, looking for a microphone so he can place an order for chili cheese fries.

There is a sign in my kitchen that reads SERVICE. I bought it as a conversation piece; an architectural statement. My son asked if that's where he should park so I can change his oil. Most guys cherish their cars—I'm just not related to any. On my first date with my husband, when push came to shove, we did. I pushed, he shoved. He looked shocked when I suggested that "E" didn't stand for "Enough." His trunk was his locker room, where he sent outgrown jocks, blown-out running shoes and mangled tennis rackets to die.

Years later, nothing has changed. Just last night, I got in his car and gagged, "What's that smell?" "Shrimp," he says. "I bought 'em fresh."

Two weeks ago.

When my son began summit negotiations with The Bob over buying t.h.e. car, I thought *Dual air bags*. His dad thought *Night job*. And his sister thought *Cute*, as in a convertible with lots and lots of cup holders. Mr. Demolition Derby demanded *Cool*.

"Cool," we learned, meant lots of letters and numbers: BMW, Z3, 2.8 liter DOHC, V-8, 227 hp, and $175,000. When he got to "chick magnet," I called a ceasefire. But father and son agreed that the most vital part of any car—after fender flares, 8 ft. tall tires or a Warn winch with an aggressive body kit—is the radio, the AM radio. An AM radio with supersonic range, so that when they drive to Antarctica they can still tune in Jim Rome on *Sports Talk*. Guys don't listen to Jim Rome, they inhale Jim Rome, they *become* Jim Rome. Primarily because they listen to him at 5,983 decibels. Unless the volume melts ear wax, shatters contact lenses or shorts out a Miracle Ear, then it's not worth listening to. It's not bad shocks that make a guy's car vibrate. It's radio activity.

As my son was pulling down the driveway the other day 25 miles over the speed limit, he slammed on the brakes and threw his arm out protectively across my chest. For a split second, after peeling my dentures off the dashboard, I thought, *He really cares*. Until I saw three girls plastered across the rear windshield.

Chick magnet, bumper car—what's the difference?

Happy Bottom Quarter

My teenaged kids are about to face one of the biggest experiences of high school. Bigger than getting arrested, trying to get a date for homecoming or piercing an appendage. They're about to encounter the SAT.

The terror of the SAT is as etched in my memory as the scars on my shins from that cute little boy kicking me every day in the third grade. Only the SAT is more painful.

I lived with a brother who was ahead of me three and a half years in age and ten light years in gray matter. For example, he actually knew what a light year was. While he excelled at worrying about grades, I excelled at worrying about whether Joan was still talking to Karen, or if Max's girlfriend Lisa knew he'd taken Sue to the drive-in, or how many cops my parents actually—horrifyingly—would hire to chaperone my first party. You know, the important stuff.

My brother, Mr. Honor Roll, told me that scoring a 1500 on the SAT was...mediocre. In his opinion, the guys who hang off the backs of garbage trucks made Bs in high school and could score a 780 verbal and 750 math, at least.

Maybe my brother thought his self-worth was subtly linked to his test scores, but I *knew* my self-worth was inextricably tied to my test scores. My parents told me so. But, I rationalized, if I didn't make a 1500, at least I'd be riding on the back of a truck...and that definitely was cool.

So when I sat down to the SAT with enough sharpened No. 2 pencils to cause lead poisoning in the entire cafeteria, I wondered if (A) the graders in Princeton, New Jersey, would give a break to a left-handed girl from Texas; (B) if it would be better to charge bribes on my dad's MasterCard or American Express; or (C) the $37.41 in my savings account would sustain me through my nursing home years. A little voice whispered, "(D) None of the above."

As I bubbled in my name, hoping that that might count for 500 points, I could've sworn I smelled garbage. I flipped to the verbal section and found analogies such as BREAD:WINNER :: TEST SCORES:SUCCESS. By the time I got to the math section, I could actually feel the sensation of hanging on to the back of a garbage truck. Forget knowing the answers—I couldn't even pronounce parts of the questions: hypotenuse, integer, obtuse, rhombus, Euclidean, $A=1/2r2~$. And what was this "pie are square" stuff? I deduced I'd been given the Greek edition.

I didn't get a score. I was told instead to consult a vegetable-stand owner because the results indicated I might be a lima bean.

I guess I'm an essay sort of gal. With some good b.s. and a shot of tequila, which I don't recall being offered at any point during the two weeks it took me to finish the SAT, I might convince those guys in Princeton that I'm more than a lima bean—I'm a garbanzo bean.

Besides, I was counting on my smart boyfriend for a successful life. But when he called to say he'd received his score—a whopping 650—I asked hopefully, "On which part?" "Total," he mumbled. At least he'd bubbled in his name correctly.

Why doesn't the SAT ask things that are pertinent in real life? Such as, in Math: If you wash four pairs of identical socks, what are the odds that three singles will march out of the dryer?

Chemistry: How do you get red wine out of white linen pants?

Reading comprehension: If Max is engaged to two women at the same time and neither one knows about the other and one of them finds out, does the death penalty still apply?

Or offer analogies a girl could relate to:

MEN:CLEAN :: (A) toilet seat:up; (B) hell:freezes over; (C) oxy:moron; (D) maid:hire.

MOTHER:CHILDREN :: (A) warden:prisoners; (B) Nurse Ratchet:inmates; (C) ventriloquist: dummy; (D) Ringling Bros.:circus animals.

My results from such a test would probably indicate: "You are safe to marry, but do not procreate."

Over time, my SAT scores improved. As I told my daughter on the eve of her life-defining test that would measure her self-worth, "Don't worry, I eked out a 1550, and look at me."

As a lifetime member of the happy bottom quarter, I'm now preparing for my next entrance exam. And if St. Peter insists on multiple choice, I'll bet Satan owns a garbage truck. Who else would have created the SAT, but SATan?

I'ds of March

Senioritis (seen-yor-eye-tis) *n.* American rite of passage to adulthood. Symptoms: inflamed ego glands induced by over-exposure to senior perks; in the female, addiction to cookie dough, chips and lip gloss; fear of looking stupid in a mortarboard, obsession with collages, tan lines and yearbook quote. Both sexes desire nagging parents to self-destruct; possess bipolar tendencies to celebrate life, preferably after curfew, while hysterical that the end is near—*SYN.* **Expensive**

Today, as every day this school year, my daughter, The Senior, and her fellow seniors will administer last rites to some piece of their high school career—the last hall pass, the last detention for an untucked shirt, the last time she'll ever be told her skirt is *too* short, the last losing season, the last mum, the last sleepover, the last dance, the last hug...the last straw.

I don't know where she thinks she's going after graduation,

but it's got to be cheaper than where she is now. As she prepares for her new life of independence, we prepare for bankruptcy.

Beware the I'ds of March. It begins with the class ring: "I'd like the Deluxe Plutonium with diamonds and lapis inlay," she said. I never saw it. It leaped off her finger the first time she washed her hands and is stuck in the drainpipe somewhere near Central America.

"I'd like to order the Super Senior Wallpaper Photo Package so I can give one to all my friends." She could give six to everyone she's ever been in school with and still have enough left over to tip the pizza delivery guys for the rest of her life. Or reward the plumber who fishes out her class ring.

"I'd like to buy a sheer, two-piece prom dress that laces up the back and down the sides with three-ounce fishing line. Oh, and highlight my hair, get a full body peel, a paraffin wax pedicure, and a French manicure."

Who could have predicted that the tomboy of two years ago—the one who thought lipstick was for writing obscene messages on her brother's bathroom mirror—would turn into Cher?

My husband muttered, "I'd like to take out a student loan to afford our student."

"And I'd like to rent a stretch limo with a hot tub in the back, a cabana boy and drink tequila shots," I shot back.

Occasionally, she acknowledges life after high school...as evidenced by her applications to 409 colleges in ten time zones. Her father offers guidance: "There's more to selecting a college than finding a school whose team colors 'bring out' your eyes, has handsome cheerleaders, or doesn't require an essay on the application. What's really important," he says, "is that you find a school that has some great golf courses nearby."

"Pebble Beach doesn't have a college," I interrupted.

"Fine, then St. Andrews..."

"Hell—lloo! Isn't that, like, in *Scotland*? I can't, like, learn, *Scotch* overnight. It's a foreign language. Besides, my friends have told me what's totally key—a dorm Starbucks, valet parking and a roommate with a shoe fetish whose brother is the campus hottie."

And to think I picked a college based on whether the dorms had indoor plumbing.

When she processes down the graduation aisle wearing an *Absolut High* T-shirt, ripped jeans and flip-flops under her $800 shantung silk graduation gown and mortarboard with gold-leaf tassels, I'll wonder, *Where did the time go?*

Amongst the long goodbyes and last rites come letters stamped *Admissions*—some thin, some not. I hold my breath and watch her fumble to open the envelopes, sitting on the bed in her room. Her room—a shrine to her protected innocence— with her yearbooks, mums and CDs; her first swim meet medal, soccer trophy and blue horse show ribbon; and a frayed copy of *Goodnight Moon,* now buried under a stack of *Seventeen* magazines. Sinking deeply into her pile of stuffed animals, I clutch her favorite pillow which smells of her and look at the hundreds of pictures thumbtacked to the walls, memorializing her now-fleeting high school career.

Her room. Her room that won't really be hers in a few months—it will be a place she only visits.

I watch as her eyes scan the first paragraph under the Admissions letterhead. She looks up at me, those eyes slowly filling with tears—a mixture of relief, fear and pride—as she reads that she gained admission into her new world. A new world that's hundreds of miles away, with only satellite parking and not a latte machine in sight. A world in which she'll learn clean underwear doesn't reproduce itself and how to decorate with pizza cartons.

In her eyes is reflected the feeling of being wanted...and the glimmer of the first goodbye.

With the possible exception of "It's a girl," no three words have so clearly and irretrievably changed our lives as "I got in."

I wish I'd seen it coming.

Kids' Treasure...Mom's Nightmare

I feel it coming...and it's not pretty. It's as predictable as the allergy season and about as welcome. An eerie sensation that waves over me like a bad rash—the itch to clean.

Each spring, I get this uncontrollable urge to hose down closet tops and drawer bottoms. An insatiable need to scrub until my knuckles bleed and my knees need replacing.

In my household, I am the Lone Ranger when it comes to cleaning. My kids hide in the landfill they call bedrooms and my husband goes into the closet, hoping he can hide his stash of favorite T-shirts—all 329 of them—from me, the T-shirt Terminator. If we could transform the stacks of T-shirts in this house into nuclear fuel, we could launch our own space station. But that would be just another place I'd feel compelled to clean each spring.

I haven't always been like this. It must be a "woman" thing.

One hundred and fifty years ago, when I was growing up in my own landfill, I was the slob living inside the department of the Neat Police. My idea of cleaning was calling maintenance.

My mother had incredibly unrealistic demands: Hands and dishes had to be washed with *soap*; dust balls larger than our schnauzer were hauled away; I couldn't use my toothbrush to comb the gerbil, and, above all, no clipping your toenails at the dinner table. She was harsh.

My father, armed at all times with a label gun, invented color-coding and the Dewey Decimal System for closets. For my 16th birthday, he gave me a key. Not to a car, but for my tube of toothpaste.

My brother has kept a daily journal since conception. He couldn't sleep until all of his pencils were sharpened and shirts hung in descending order of the color spectrum. I figured all men were like this until I married a confirmed bachelor who kept his blankets in the microwave, had ketchup predating the

Civil War and saved the pieces of toilet paper commemorating his first shaving experience.

Somewhere between puberty and having to file my own tax return, I gave birth to my mother. I couldn't help it. It was hormonal. It was survival instinct. I went from acting like Sandra Dee to worshiping Leona Helmsley—mistress of my own housekeeping-from-hell destiny.

Now that I'm blessed with kids whose rooms accumulate enough dirt to mulch the back 40—if we had a back 40—I again wish I could call maintenance.

As a seasoned cleaning veteran, I take my life in my own hands and journey once a year into the kids' landfill. But, first, I attach a nose clamp. In the middle of the room usually sits a piece of modern art —a car wreck—which, in reality, is a mound of dirty clothes and wet towels welded together with Mars bars and Bazooka bubble gum.

I wade through used Band-Aids, old ticket stubs and matchbook collections. I find drawers full of the torn edges to computer grade sheets, but no report cards. Behind Door No. 1 is every *Sports Illustrated/Glamour* magazine since their births which have since hatched 1,219 generations of cockroaches. And counting.

In a bold move, I decided to make my son take responsibility. Trying to turn him into a Renaissance man, I asked him to clean the toilet.

He put the seat down...after tossing a Molatov cocktail inside. I handed him an iron; he made a grilled cheese. I plugged in the Hoover; he vacuumed the dirty dishes.

I would've asked him to change his sheets, but what's the point? He sleeps in his clothes.

There are some signs of hope. I smelled Right Guard in his room the other day, which evidently he used for air freshener. When there's no time to shower, he's found a few squirts of Windex will do. I'd give him a candle to burn, but if he closed the door, we might all go up in flames.

When I get serious about cleaning, I guess I'll do what my mother did.

Run away.

Backing into Manhood

There are so many times in a boy's life when he must look in the mirror and respond to the call to be a man. The first time he ties a tie, needs to apply a tourniquet around his neck to stop the bleeding from shaving, and parallel parks.

If my son is lucky, there probably will be a woman around somewhere who will eagerly assist him with the first two. Trying to maneuver a car sideways into a space the length of a baseball bat wasn't even all that tricky—give a fender or two. Not nearly as tricky as, say, backing out of the driveway.

Over breakfast one morning, I tried to impress upon him, when he was a man, the value of history—how much we can learn looking back on past mistakes and apply to one's future... as he moves forward.

"Got it, mom." Before slamming the door, he said, "Peace out," and was gone.

Could it really have been only minutes later (or light years?) that, standing in my kitchen, my first cup of coffee halfway to my lips, I heard it. Crash, crunch, screech—not necessarily in that order.

The only sound louder than the din of crumpling steel was the soar of rising insurance rates.

Kicking myself (in hindsight, of course), I realized that an abstract lesson on the past didn't mean squat to a sixteen-year-old. I mean, what was I thinking? What's there for him to look back on other than puberty? What I'd glossed over was the more practical side—such as looking back literally, using a rearview mirror.

Our son had backed into a car...parked behind him. In our driveway.

It was bad enough that this happened on my husband's birthday, but the real sting was the car's owner was our next-door neighbor. As in, Best-Man-in-our-wedding, the sucker who'd been conned into thinking loaning us his car was an okay idea.

What it was was a guy idea.

A woman would never borrow a neighbor's car. Not just because of, jeez, someone might dent it and then there would be something called a friendship that could be damaged. No, I would never borrow a car from a friend, because if a minute scratch appeared, she'd know where I live.

It wasn't a car wreck that would make the news. But it was a make-a-man moment: telling someone who'd known him practically before his parents did that his car was several inches shorter than when he'd last seen it.

"It's called a 'growth opportunity,'" I said. Little did he know that when he got an estimate for the body repairs he'd be paying for, his next growth opportunity would be called "working your ass off."

Mysteriously, his father had failed to mention to him that he'd once backed into a car parked behind him. Meaning what—it's genetic?

He'd backed into my stepsister's car. In our driveway. With his perplexed business partner sitting in the passenger seat looking in his side view mirror, trying to envision how Wonder Boy was going to get around the car parked directly behind him.

Facing the music squarely with honesty and integrity, my husband marched into our house, looked my stepsister straight in the eye and said, "Toss me your keys. I need to move your car."

No confession. No remorse. Just a Clinton-esque swagger. His excuse was—and this will come as a tremendous shock— he had a tee time.

So, nobody's perfect.

Searching for solitude, I took my car to the gas station, filled it up and splurged on a really bad car wash. Sitting in my driver's seat, the suds about to blast, I glanced in my sideview mirror (the one that's splintered in a million pieces by a mis-fired lacrosse ball thrown, where else, in my driveway). I blanched—the door to my gas tank was open. I jumped out to shut it and discovered I'd also failed to screw the cap back on. Another nanosecond and...

Later, while I was waiting in line to rent a car for our Best Man, with caked carwash suds in my hair and bristle marks running down one side of my still-damp sweat suit, I saw a woman whose face was the color of week-old milk. I recognized the tick in her cheek.

"My son had a wreck," she choked.

I nodded that maternal "been there" nod.

"I worry about him every time he pulls out of the driveway," she groaned.

Lucky duck. At least, her son makes it out of the driveway.

Searching my eyes for some kind of understanding, she continued, "You know, it's true—most accidents occur within a mile from the home."

Or closer, in some cases. All I could muster was, "We both should move."

Don't Hold Your Breath

I've located the source of destruction of the ozone layer. My son's lacrosse gear.

Most of the time, his equipment is locked inside his car, marinating in sweat and heat—petrified, potent and poisonous—the finger of aroma wafting out, poking innocent passersby between the eyes.

Aroma...what am I saying? It's more like a heady blend of year-old milk and mustard gas; like Pepe and the entire LePew family are having a reunion under his seats.

Armed with goggles, kitchen mitts and tongs, my husband, daughter and I surrounded his car like a S.W.A.T. team. "You! Pop open the rear door. You! Cover the sides," I barked through the towel over my mouth.

On cue, we flung open all the doors to find...more layers than a geological dig. Buried under books were fossilized jockstraps, paralyzed pads and remnants of Supersized Beltbuster meals oozing ketchup. And it was all turning to mulch. The rust stain under his car wasn't rust after all. It was a slow leak of Heinz 57.

In our laundry room stood his lacrosse uniform in Stage 4 rigor mortis, suspended without a hanger. Its sleeves, like arms, were outstretched, begging to be washed.

Shocked, I took a deep breath...then thought better of it. Should I use embalming fluid, 20 Mule Team Borax™ or hang it outside as a bug zapper?

"How long has it been since you washed your uniform?" I shrieked. Silence...right response, wrong question.

"Okay, how long has it been since your uniform was washed?"

"I dunno...the beginning of the season?"

"Which season...deer or holiday?!" Again, silence.

"Okay, which year?" I hollered.

"The school's only had a team two years."

And there it was. The answer: two years without one drop of disinfectant. Wonder how long it's been since the road warrior himself saw soap? The Super Bowl?

"It's my lucky uniform."

"It's your only uniform. Who's going to do your laundry in college?"

"My girlfriend."

"Unless she breathes through her ears, she'll never last."

"Mom, the season's almost over. Lemme just turn it in next week. They'll never know."

"What...and asphyxiate the next kid?"

As I drew him a map to the laundry room, he asked, "What temperature setting do I set the water on?"

"What does it say on the jersey?

"Parsley."

At his last game, I don't know which overpowered the opponents more: our guys' collective odor...or playing like champions.

Immersed in the thrill of an underdog victory, my boy stood on the sidelines with a smile that beamed a thousand words. I was overcome—for once, not by fumes. In the parking lot, away from where any teammates could see, he threw his arms around me, drenching me, my sweater...and my heart.

To the year-end sports banquet, his last one, he wore a tie and camel hair jacket...the one he'd bought for a buck, that looked like he'd pressed it with his tongue.

Moving proudly through the crowd, he slapped hands with his teammates, the brothers he never had. All were dressed, most showered, looking like the champions they'd proven themselves to be.

As my son's name was called, he stood, a dried spaghetti noodle clinging to his jacket. His co-captain and best friend stood next to him, a French fry hanging from his tie—probably from the back seat of my son's car.

I stood in the rear of the room, alone. Partly because I was still wearing the sweater that smelled of him. Partly to let the last four years wash over me. But mainly, trying to figure out when he'd become a man.

If you ever get close enough to me, you'll know the sweater—it will smell of a season most memorable.

A season that lasted eighteen years.

Communication for Dummies

When my kids were babies, I instinctively understood each gurgle, coo and spit-up. I knew the difference between a cry of hunger and, say, falling off the kitchen counter. I alone held the secret decoder: "bops" were grapes; "gucky" was blanket; and "beppy" meant "The Coke in my bottle is flat."

Unfortunately, I haven't understood a word they've said since. Even when I understood the words, I still needed someone to explain, "Jeez, it's like, you know, whatever."

Then came Instant Message.

A box on my computer screen would pop up: "waddup." Not having a clue who TequilaTexan is, I'd key in, "Nothing." The reply: "kewl." This insightful banter continued until I realized it was my sixth-grader IM-ing me...from the next room.

My college kids aren't much better. Boxes have popped up, "wuz a cuncushen feel like?" and "hav the campus police called u yet?" When I respond with my own question, "How are classes?" they log off and I hear the sound of a door slamming in my face. It's like they never left home.

Other than streaking, sacrificing a goat, and duct-taping

kids inside their dorm rooms, I'm not sure what aspect of higher education college offers. Not English—theirs is a generation of e.e. cummings meets Samuel Morse.

When my oldest daughter is home from college, our banter is more like Twenty Questions—me, trying to entice her into something called a conversation. So far, she has not fallen for that old trick.

"Where are you going?" I ask. Which, of course, leads to, "Would a little blush kill you?" "Do you want me to put some makeup on that thing?" "Are you trying to starve yourself?" "You sound like you've gained a few pounds." "You're wearing those with that?" "You sure that zipper goes in the front?" "What can I say? You have your dad's eyebrows." "Exactly how many natural colors are in the hair spectrum?" "Did you wear that to lunch with your grandmother?" "A woman should put a little effort into how she looks." "You shouldn't care so much about how you look." "You're an adult." "Why the hurry to grow up?" "You're on your own."

"Is that a Cheerio stuck in your belly button...or a navel ring?" "Do all your dates look like Charles Manson/act like John Belushi/eat like that?" "How can a tattoo be temporary?" "Your hair is so pretty, you should wear it down." "You need a haircut." "You look pale." "Any more sun and you'll be dancing the lead with the California Raisins." "Don't talk with your mouth full. Speak up. What, you're *choking*? Put on some lipstick—the paramedic might be single."

"I'm not being critical, but if you'd style your hair, work out, quit hemming your clothes with pinking shears, stop biting your nails, whiten your teeth, wear a WonderBra, get new glasses, eat more fiber, read the *Wall Street Journal*, take smaller bites, smile more, be less judgmental, dare to be different, conform, lower your standards, raise your sights...don't interrupt...I forgot what I was saying..."

Mothers of sons already know how conversations go with

them. They don't. A boy—say, mine—might, one minute, be standing in front of the refrigerator in his boxers; the next, be out the door.

"Later," he shouts. "Going to Austin."

"Wait, don't you need...shoes?" He gives me that blank look—the permanent one—that says, "Huh?"

Taking the stairs three at a time, he runs to his room. Thundering back down wearing one high top and a flip-flop, he lunges for the back door.

"Shirt?" I query, as he passes. "Oh, yeah." Again, back upstairs and back down.

"Wallet?" I ask, not even looking up. "Oh, yeah."

After thirteen "oh, yeah" trips up and down, he finally gets in the car, backs down the driveway...and ran out of gas.

I had high hopes for my last child, but even at twelve years old, it's not looking too good.

"I'm going out," she starts.

"Where?"

"Not where. Who."

"Who what?"

"Asked me out."

"Where?"

"On the phone."

"How do you go out on the phone?"

"I didn't."

"So, you're not going out."

"Yes, I am."

"With who?"

"It's whom."

"Who's whom?"

"When?"

"When what?"

"When are you going out?"

"Where?"

"I don't know where. You won't tell me."

The phone rings. She runs to caller ID. "It's him," she screams.

"Him who?"

"You know, the one. 'Out' him...the phone!?"

"You're outing someone on the phone?"

Let's review. My 12-year-old daughter is going out, but not really, with someone named Him Who. Or is it Him One? Maybe Him Phone. Which means we need more. Phones. Which is never for me. And until I find out what she just said, she's grounded. Not that she was going out in the first place.

Like E.coli on room-temp pork, this communication thing is starting to grow on me.

A Walk in the Woulds

With our daughter home from college, our family intact once again, the focus, at least for the first weekend, was on our son's graduation. Having experienced back-to-back years with a graduating senior, I begin to think that Sisyphus is no Greek myth, but perhaps a patron saint for parents...and teachers. Each of us forever pushing a huge rock up a mountain, only to have it—upon reaching the top—roll down again.

As I watched my son process with his classmates in a sea of green, tasseled caps and gowns, the energy it took to get him to the top of the mountain washed over me.

Seventeen years of gnashing teeth over the definition of "decent"...as in clothes, music and behavior.

Fifteen years of carpooling, the final six with a paper bag over my head, earplugs and a muzzle.

Ten years of surviving one phone line, answering it faithfully, knowing that the only time it was for me was when Caller ID read "obscene."

Five years of editing term papers at 3 a.m., when I didn't have the gray matter to understand the subject matter.

Two and half years of wondering how far "empty" will take him; worrying each time he peeled out of the driveway, holding our breaths until he screeched back in.

$235,854 later—three broken arms; six outpatient surgeries; five clay handprints; 20 baby teeth; two funerals: a dog and a grandfather—both man's best friend; sixteen Mother's Day cards; one pair of training wheels; eleven broken windows; two SATs; 139 tutorial hours; 13,789 loads of laundry; $18\frac{1}{2}$ years of laughter, tears, love, hate, fighting, and forgiving...

And nine months of letting go as we watch each "last" moment slip by...we have successfully rolled the Sisyphean rock to the top of the mountain.

As a teenager, I was cautioned about the wisdom of falling in love with someone's potential. As a mother, it's the desire to see that potential filled that gets me out of bed every morning. Particularly one who is the class clown.

As my son approached the commencement stage to receive his diploma, I was thunderstruck: *What did he just put in his mouth?* Under his bulging lips, he'd slipped huge, plastic, hillbilly "Bubba" teeth.

Only an accidental moment of grace could explain why he glanced over at me, our eyes locking. My laser-like glare, a direct hit. Buckling like Superman drilled with Kryptonite, he—albeit reticently—took out the plastic teeth and shoved them into his pocket. With a "seconds-from-a-clean-getaway" grin, he crossed the stage, returning to his seat...a graduate.

In the blink of an eye, the last four years are filed into our repository of time. Irreplaceable moments, now memories— sound bites from the glory days ranging from hilarity to make-a-man moments.

Hidden tears within, I let go...each "last" high school experience silently transforming into anxious heartbeats of what's to come. Reflecting on what was, we look to what will be.

On the teachers, the men and women adorned in gowns of black and jewel-toned hoods, a special document of honor should be conferred. While we provided support, they connected the dots, outlining boys-to-men, giving them the tools to color in with their dreams. Our task, a labor of love; theirs, an answer to a higher call.

Believing in potential—of what "could" be—I handed my son to them. On their walk together, potential blossomed into purpose...and he has emerged full of what "would" be. The teachers, having achieved their goal yet another year, remain behind to push the next class up the mountain.

My son turns now to college—and I turn to my youngest child—but first, I will relish the temporary respite of my walk back down the mountain.

Window Seat of Opportunity

My daughter wanted me to go with her. Well, that's what she said...three months ago. "Pulleezze be a chaperone on my bus to camp," she begged. So I did, knowing that—given that she's almost 12 and all—it may be my last window of opportunity to be with her. Soon, she'll prefer that I be under the bus.

So, three months ago she was excited. Even that morning, as I cut the crust off her pb&j sandwich for the five-hour bus trip, she was excited.

But when we arrived at the bus and she saw her friends, it was obvious—next to not shaving your legs, having your mother on your bus to camp could be the biggest popularity killer in life. My role from that point on was to wear a blanket over my head.

It's not her fault. She's hit the age when a girl realizes that the entire world is against her...which is so totally obvious, given how dumb parents have become since breakfast. It's when angels turn to she-devils, launching into tears over the wrong face wash or wrong colored/flavored lip-gloss. It's a hormone trip created by God that happens to coincide with—and this is really, really funny—my hormone trip. That God, I tell you—what a sense of humor.

I know it won't last forever. It just feels like it.

Flanking either side of the camp buses were hundreds of parents, all heartbroken and crying goodbye to their daughters. The dads were holding their sides from carrying their daughters' trunks built like Hummers; while the mothers, who were dressed better at 7:15 a.m. than I would be to accept the Pulitzer Prize or Pillsbury Bake-off blue ribbon, were waving to the little darlings who had staked out the prime window seats at 4:00 that morning.

I was sweating profusely from hauling my daughter's duffel bag that held her rock collection; the complete set of the *Mary Kate and Ashley Encyclopedia of Skits, Fingernail Art and Hair Braiding*; and her microwave/refrigerator.

When I went to camp, I was gone for eight weeks, and all I took was a flashlight and a map home. Of course, that was a long time ago when we couldn't bring even a transistor radio—in part because they hadn't been invented. We also were supposed to be "roughing it." Girls today have Bose headphones for their Walkmans, Discmans and DVD players. To them, "roughing it" means leaving their cell phones at home.

We both had high hopes for her time at camp.

I hoped my daughter would learn how to build a campfire, short-sheet beds and live with a broken nail. I'd told her all about my camp days where we went on overnights in the wilderness, ate dry cereal and hid our food from bears. We never had a dance; therefore, we never showered or brushed our hair. And we kept pet mice in our pockets.

She hoped Tribe Hill didn't fall on the same night as *American Idol.*

I followed her onto her bus. She turned around and whispered, "No, Mom. You're on that bus," pointing to the one behind her. "They need a chaperone—they're ten-year-olds."

As I felt the whoosh of air in my face as the bus door shut between us, I felt that window of opportunity closing as well.

It marked the beginning of our hormone trips in opposite directions—hers coming, mine going. I know we'll meet again someday, only we'll be older, maybe wiser. And I, no doubt, will still be crazy...after all those years.

S'mores to the Soul

When I was ten years old, I spent many rest periods on my upper bunk in a cabin that smelled of old wood, damp towels and timeworn mattresses. Eight weeks was a long time never to cut your fingernails, avoid public showers and wear only three shirts. With pen in hand, I'd peer out the window at the Sangre de Cristo mountains of New Mexico and wonder—if my parents won't come get me, can I find my way home on my own?

Bears permitting.

As the weeks wore on, I memorized the recipe for bug

juice, the directions for folding the perfect hospital corner, and the techniques for mastering tetherball. I learned the simple physical pleasures of riding a horse, had rowdy sing-alongs in the dining hall, and giggled into my pillowcase long after Taps. Tribes competed to win, but with a stack of yellow, green and pink ribbons in my trunk, I never felt I'd lost; I felt only pig-in-slop-joy that I'd been a part.

By camp's end, the quiet tears of unspoken fear I shed on my arrival turned into convulsing sobs of having to say good-bye at camp closing.

Since then, my idea of camping has devolved into guaranteed reservations at Motel 6. But the camps my kids attended offered greater challenges. My oldest daughter has stood atop a 13,000-foot peak and felt the power of a towering cloudscape. She's slept under a canopy of stars on a backpack, flown down a snowfield on her backside, and learned 13 different ways to eat chicken out of a can—a survival skill that came in handy in college when she lived with no meal plan.

My son's first camp experience was a re-enactment of *Lord of the Flies*—without society (or, in his case, sober counselors) a boy can cover up his inner savagery for only so long before it breaks out. "I thought you said camp was fun," he'd write. But somewhere in that state of madness, between foraging for food in the camp kitchen and realizing that bathing was a total loser-waste-of–time, he came to rely on himself. Of course, perfecting the art of making a blowtorch with a can of Lysol and a Bic lighter wasn't too shabby, either. Judging from the charred framework of the Animal House he lives in at college, he's used that survival skill on more than one occasion...to the chagrin of the local Volunteer Fire Department.

His coming-of-age developed at later camps—sitting in the stern of a canoe, riding a zip-line, leading his group of sea-kayakers with only a compass and a conscience. Hiking with others, learning to pitch a tent and build a campfire, he, as his sister before him, discovered nature...as well as the nature of others.

He's been a character all his life, but his string of summers provided character of another kind. A mother's hope is that it will be the self-reliant thing, not the not-bathing thing, that will stick with him.

My youngest child has eluded canned chicken and blow-torches. At least, thus far. Her experiences have been steeped in the Kum-ba-ya nature of skit night, War Canoe, campfire talks and laughing like she's never laughed before. For her, forging lifelong friendships...well, it doesn't get better than that.

Anxiously entering high school, she'll have to step outside her comfort zone. But having had a front-row seat to her sister's and brother's exploits—from the chinks in their armor to the way they lived the life of Riley—she knows that she can't let stepping into unknown waters tip her balance. She built confidence around that campfire and learned that where you're coming from is not nearly as important as where you're going.

As August's heavy, sultry air takes the curl out of my world, I am the one who most dreads the end of summer—its lazy mornings, afternoons open to interpretation and relaxed, late-night dinners. I hate leaving the familiar banks of the river at our summer house to dip our toes into the unfamiliar waters that lie ahead—new school, new job in a new city, new stories to write—my bears in the woods.

What I learned under the watch of the Sangre de Cristo mountains was underscored by my daughter's barely-misty eyes at her camp closing—if we don't let go of one great adventure, we'll miss the next.

Camp is not life, but it's a good foundation. Pressed between the pages of homesickness, independence and team spirit, life lessons stick like s'mores to the soul. Bears in the woods notwithstanding, recalling the days of name tags in my clothes, pen in hand, I realize I have found my way home.

The Red Army

At the height of the Cold War in the '60s, while the world was focused on the Bay of Pigs, I struggled with my own global powers: Cheryl, Tina and Diane. They may have been only nine years old and in the fifth grade, but they dominated my world...as well as every other girl's world in my class.

The girls in my class fell into two categories: the Red Army—who advanced into our lives dictating what we were to think and do—and everyone else. Khrushchev banged his shoe. Cheryl, Tina and Diane stole mine to use in a friendly game of keep-away. Their trade embargo loomed larger than the Berlin Wall, preventing me from passing notes to my best friend (make that, only friend) Nancy. Just their whispers and steel-eyed glances could freeze me and my cooties away from the lunchroom table, birthday party or kickball game—the axes of life.

Like a string of paper dolls, they talked alike, had the same haircut, and all got to wear patent leather Mary Jane shoes to school.

With the social savvy of a dung beetle, I wore corrective shoes. I had one eyebrow that stretched from one side of my face to the other. And I brought a sack lunch to school every day. Tuna fish. Getting head lice would've improved my ranking in the fifth-grade food chain.

I never understood why they didn't like me. Were they jealous that I made 100s on my spelling tests? Won arm-wrestling contests? Or was it because I could fake a pretty convincing seizure? (The same loser attribute I used pathetically to attract guys later, but that's another story.)

But when you're ten and your toes turn in and kids call you "unibrow" and you smell like week-old canned tuna, how are you supposed to know that their venomous personal attacks weren't personal at all? That their words said more about them than they did about...me?

The cold wars accelerated in middle school. I didn't own one pair of Pappagallos, a Bermuda bag with wooden handles, not even a headband. The Red Army proved their superiority by lifting an eyebrow, flipping their board-straight hair and wrapping their forefinger and thumb around their wrists, proving that thin wins. All I could prove was that I was double-jointed, pulling my thumb backwards until something popped.

Real revenge, I heard, would be mine if I cut out their yearbook pictures, put them in ice cube trays and froze them. But I wasn't willing to ruin my yearbook.

With time, the Red Army eventually disbanded. They were either squeezed out or, hitting their zenith in eighth, tenth, twelfth grade...flamed out like shooting stars.

Unfortunately, they were replaced by other cells of female terrorists—college cliques, favored bridesmaids, new mothers with flawless pregnancies and perfect children, league tennis and ladies day on the golf course. Fortunately, I've learned to recognize the army long before it advances...and now I run the other way.

But when I saw familiar tears welling in my daughter's eyes, my own eyes burned with empathy and memories of just how mean mean-girls could be.

She wasn't ten, but almost 16—a time when it means everything to be accepted. Aiming poison-tipped words at her back, a new "friend" (a veritable stranger) had shot her down as she moved in on my daughter's oldest friend, purposefully stealing a piece of her heart. The piece once belonging to my daughter. My daughter's fragile pain was as palpable as my own stomach being put through a paper shredder.

Having never run with Prom Kings or Drama Queens, I considered—for the briefest of moments—telling her about when I tried out for cheerleader, fell on my keister in front of the entire school, and got laughed out of the auditorium...and

I turned out all right.

But I stopped myself, realizing that, at her age, the only thing worse than being given the fatal cootie diagnosis is being told you could turn out like your mother.

Piled on top of my bed, arms and legs entangled, I told her instead about the Red Army. We shared a few tears until, worn out, our emotional pendulum swayed to the great equalizer—laughter.

Together, we concluded that sometimes being picked on is a good thing. When singled out, we're presented the opportunity to dig deep and hopefully find the strength to stand on our own.

In between hugs and shooting wadded-up tissues into the wastebasket, I did my best to assure her that the best is yet to come. Armed with these experiences, she is marching down the road to herself...to that better someone on the other side.

As she crawled down from my bed, I actually heard myself saying the same words my mother said to me (the mother I never wanted to emulate). We are put here not to judge differences, but accept them, share our gifts, and somehow make this world a better place.

The Red Army might've possessed the verbal nuclear weapons to temporarily destroy my world, but they lacked what it takes to compete as a true world power.

Tender mercy.

Letting Go

After years of clinging to their lives, the steering wheel and my sanity, the deepest, darkest secret of motherhood raised its ugly head—my real job was no longer comparing, driving or even holding on. It was letting go. Freeing them to pursue their own dreams, their own lives.

As they tried on grown-up lives, I watched a revolving door of love interests come and go. Trying to keep my mouth shut, some days I was more successful than others.

I learned not to ask my daughter where her blue-eyed, blond-haired hottie went to high school...because there was no guarantee he did.

I did not ask my son's Harley chick—the one with so many piercings I feared she'd spring a leak—who she voted for, because maybe her felony status prevented her from doing so.

And when my youngest introduced me to an older man of 19 years with $3/4$ sleeves (as in almost-arm's-length tattoos), she announced proudly, "Mom! He does community service!." I did not ask if it was part of his parole.

So, now when I throw up my hands, it's either to pray for rain or signal a Hail Mary. Because while I've given them the knowledge, faith and security to run the length of the field and rack up as many points on the scoreboard as they choose, once you're a parent, you never get to spike the football.

With their first chapters of life under their belts, their stories continue to unfold, their endings defined not by our dreams, but by their own purpose.

After the wringing of hands over finding the right pre-school, SAT tutor, and whether the differences in The Bob's and my religions and metabolisms retarded or spurred them on, I cut myself some slack, knowing that I did the best I could. Who they are and ultimately who they will become is part genetic, part karmic/manic/psychic/toxic/frenetic, but, to me, it's 100% magnetic.

After fretting over their choice of friends ("Do they lift you up?"), if they really had assigned designated drivers ("Call me, no questions asked") and defining "success," this is what a mother's ultimate dream comes down to: Stay alive.

As my writing material grew up, I stepped outside my bubble, seeking new fodder. My eyes were widened by those who live less than charmed lives, who have never known what it feels like to be safe, secure, cared for...who die too young. Slowly, as I redirected my focus outward from my children, mankind became my fascination.

I have entered circles into which I never would have gained access had someone not labeled me a "writer." Time after time, I have been exposed to everyday angels, seen goodness in dark places, and witnessed miracles that, without enlightenment from my past, would have gone unrecognized.

I visited homeless shelters and befriended addicts on their road to recovery; schools, where teachers brought imagination and intellect to life; and hospitals where nurses and volunteers provided comfort and joy. I held trembling hands, released balloons at childhood grief centers, and saw hope. I went to overnight pediatric cancer camps, painted bald heads with smiley faces, jumped on rolling IV poles like a skateboard...and shared laughter; to jails, and witnessed forgiveness melting walls of ice on the inside. I participated alongside Special Olympians who, with their special brand of courage, revealed the quality of mind, if not body, which enables them to face hardship resolutely.

For all these people, success cannot be measured by the points on the scoreboard. Success is in the attempt.

In doing so, they touch greatness. In touching greatness, they inspire greatness in those around them. Tapping into a well beyond the spring of motherhood, they also helped me find the other part of myself.

The entire time, I thought my kids weren't looking. Funny, how they, too, had eyes in the backs of their heads.

Running Away...Home

It was one of those days I wished I had a closet—that could be locked from the inside. One of those days when I'd been assaulted from all directions—the First Church of Chuck Norris soliciting converts, the Marijuana Political Party in need of a match, a clothing donation for women CEOs. Everyone wanting something I wasn't interested in, couldn't find or didn't have.

Then, I got a call from our coed daughter who'd been dealt an unexpected blow.

It was not a life-threatening blow. In the grand scheme of life, an outsider might have classified it under "hangnail." While I knew this, too, would pass, I also knew it had cut her to the core, exposing a piece of self-esteem that had never been threatened.

Another growth opportunity.

In her voice was the unspoken: too independent to need a shoulder, but not bulletproof. So, I did what mothers do.

I ran away from home. And ran to her.

A feat that was not exactly facilitated by airport security. Holding a last-minute ticket and my Hefty trash bag carry-on, I was definitely tagged "high-level security risk," as if my tennis shoe laces were fuses.

After disrobing at the first security check to the extent I thought they'd offer to do my laundry, I got clearance...for about 3 feet. Then I was awarded a full body search conducted by King Kong in latex gloves. Meanwhile, unsuspicious passengers passed undeterred, boarding with their goats.

I sat next to a young mother holding her baby in one arm and restraining her toddler with the other three. As we backed away from the gate, the little girl began screaming "Dad-dy, Dad-dy, Daaad-dy!" choking on gulps of recycled air, not stopping until she and her mom deplaned two hours later.

Doing my own deep breathing during a short stopover, the next group of passengers boarded. My new seatmates—a dad and his little boy, who, for the next hour, screamed, "I want my Mooomm-my!"

Therein lies just one of the rubs of parenthood: If only one parent can be present, it is always the wrong one. A phenomenon driven home hours later when, after arriving on my daughter's campus and surprising her, the first thing she asked was, "Where's Dad?"

We mused on meaningless things, forcing laughter, until she felt like talking. I felt like Wilson, the battered, bloodied volleyball in *Cast Away*, offering silent companionship until she was strong enough to battle the seas on her own. What I'd under-estimated was how quickly her inner strength had garnered her wind within...she'd already set sail before I even arrived.

On my flight home, security had downgraded me to a mere "minimum embarrassment risk" (note to self: check cowboy boots for trailing toilet paper when leaving ladies room). I snared a seat next to a quiet-looking, older woman absorbed in her book, hoping she wouldn't want to talk.

I shut my eyes, mentally dissecting my daughter's hangnail—now my open wound. As a Mama Bear, I was keeping busy listing the many ways I would never get vengeance on the girls who had consciously shut out my daughter. In a strange Freudian/Woody Allen twist, my daughter grasped before I did that, with girls like that as members, she'd never want to be a member anyway.

I felt the woman close her book and watched with one eye open as she fumbled for something in her purse. She pulled out a rosary.

Great. Either she knew something unpleasant about this flight that I didn't or she was about to inquire into the state of my soul—either one would be a definite conversation-stopper.

Her quivering fingers moved clumsily over the beads as her thin, pale lips mouthed prayers. Her heart, seeking comfort. Catching my eye, she said almost apologetically, "It's been a while since I've used these," clutching her beads. I nodded, stone-faced, wanting to get back to the hangnail.

"My daughter was just diagnosed with cancer," she said above a whisper. "Stage Four." Her oversized words had trouble squeezing into her pocket-sized voice. "I feel a bit like a runaway, just dropping everything at home to be with her."

It might be possible to feel smaller than I did at that moment, but I doubt it. Unless I was in her shoes.

With nothing to render but a soft nod acknowledging a mother's worst fear, I listened as she talked. Digging down, deep within, while looking up, she fell silent...there were no words left to say.

We sat together, just a couple of mothers, two hearts facing miles-apart growth opportunities, knowing instinctively that if home is where the heart is, we hadn't run away at all.

We'd run right to it.

Here's to You, Mrs. Robinson

Recently, I had the opportunity to sit in on one of my daughter's college lectures. Opportunity, not invitation. Unless begging her counts—and showing her a copy of who paid her tuition.

"Okay, fine," she acquiesced. "But promise you won't speak to me or my friends, and you'll have to pretend to be someone else's mother." Since that didn't differ from any other day of motherhood, I walked the opposite way across campus.

Entering the lecture hall, I'd never seen so many attractive young people. And they were all my age! At least, through my eyes. But for my control top pantyhose, Jaclyn Smith elastic-waist pants and half-glasses, I thought I blended right in.

"Sit over there, next to Nicole. Nicole Robinson," my daughter hissed. "Act like you're her mother. And don't look at me."

Nicole was a 6' tall, blue-eyed redhead whose name could be Kidman. I was so flattered that my daughter thought I could actually pull off being her mother. I mean, being a 5'5" blood-shot blonde, on a good day I might be confused with Nicole Kidman's dog walker.

I nestled in between Nicole and a good-looking, muscular young man to whom I politely introduced myself, sparing him the later embarrassment of confusing me for, say, his date that weekend.

Remembering I was supposed to be Nicole's mother, I said, "Hi, I'm Mrs. Robinson," at which point, Paul Simon began singing in my ear, "Coo-coo-ca-choo."

The course was the Civil War; the professor, a bow-tied, tweed-jacketed, white-haired, vintage Southern scholar, straight out of *The Paper Chase*. Of course, there was no danger of anyone else in the room noting that similarity because, from their youthful perspective, that TV show was produced during the Civil War.

In fact, I imagine that most of my fellow students assumed I'd been produced during the Civil War, too.

Hearing this distinguished professor speak, I was thrown back to my own college days—all the old, familiar feelings pouring over me. Being a left-hander contortedly writing upside down on a right-handed pull-out desk...and nausea. Once again, I'd come to class unprepared and knew I'd blow the final. I felt hung over—from a fraternity party 25 years ago.

Riveted, I couldn't take my eyes off the professor. Which is fortunate since the professor never took his eyes off me—he was equally riveted that I—anyone—was taking notes. Not that he would have been particularly impressed had he seen that I was just jotting down a reminder of where I'd parked my car.

But he did appear comforted when referencing the Viet Nam war that there was at least one pair of eyes that didn't say, "Was that like before the Trojan War or after?"

Unfortunately, three minutes into the lecture my undiagnosed ADD unleashed, and I searched the audience to see if anyone might sell me some Ritalin.

A few students were slightly less riveted than I. Such as the ripped young man next to me—in a coma, his head on my shoulder, drooling. Only a mother could consider this a public display of affection. And one girl was reading *The Worst-Case Scenario Survival Handbook: Dating*—the chapter entitled, "Is Your Date an Axe Murderer?"

At this point, the professor began to describe with distinct euphoria an 1862 incident in which a Mr. Landringham—when demonstrating in court how someone could, in fact, shoot himself in his own back—shot and killed himself in his own back.

At least, that's what my notes say. I was too consumed wondering if Mr. Landringham was an ancestor to dear Mrs. Landringham, the late secretary on *West Wing.*

Everyone perked up when the professor began discussing *Ex Parte* members, taking that as a sign that class was over, as in "Time to Par-tay." No matter that it was 11 a.m. Monday.

As class dispersed, I hugged my daughter—and Nicole—goodbye. Trying gently to let down both the professor and my good-looking, ripped-but-drooling true love, I told them both that I'd be back. For the latter, I'd bring a towel.

Paul Simon still singing in my ear, I returned home with enough fear to fill the next several decades with continuing nightmares of facing a final...in a course I went to only once.

Mr. & Mrs. Last Resort

"You're doing *what* for spring break?!" my doctor friend Melanie shrieked.

"Taking my son and four other seniors to South Padre Island," I repeated, cringing in disbelief. She wrote out a prescription for Atavan. "And don't mix it with scotch," she cautioned.

It wasn't my idea. Padre, that is. The Atavan and scotch would've occurred to me eventually.

Rewind to February. My son, the one who hasn't touched me since he discovered cooties, put his arm around me. "Yo, Mom. None-of-the-other-parents'll-go-so-I-told-the-guys-you-n-dad'd-take-us-to-Cancun," he stated, squeezing me senseless.

Color us "Mr. & Mrs. Last Resort." But, Cancun? Why not Boys Town? Or Sodom and Gomorrah? "Mr. & Mrs. Last Rites" didn't occur to me until after we'd compromised on Padre and were heading south.

Ah, South Padre. Where collegiate scholars go to recover from the one book they've read all year...other than *Playboy*. Where they let it all hang out—of windows, bathing suits, and the backs of police cars. The land of bleach-tipped, spiked hair; Budweiser; and beauties basting belly-up. Boys, bereft of their senses, bond with their binoculars in bull sessions of bottomless bravura.

Where just one week before we arrived, there'd been only one murder and rape, but several hundred beatings and wet T-shirt contests. Given how many girls considered T-shirts optional, I thought maybe some mobile unit was offering free mammograms down the beach.

The island, like its inhabitants, was constantly enveloped in a haze. Possibly due to the 52,987 cars crossing the one-lane bridge from the mainland to the holy land. It was like vacationing on an L.A. freeway during rush hour, carbon monoxide the drug of choice.

Only a few (say 35,463) reveled on the beach, each connected to a video camera, cell phone and, for life support, Marlboros and a beer bong. Many were connected to one another; all working diligently to reduce their brain cells to a more manageable size, which was bound to be lower than their number of body piercings, tattoos of religious icons (J Lo, Mike Tyson) and tallboys in their Igloo.

While the rest of the world was observing Lent, the concept of "sacrifice" apparently never made it this far south. Spring Breakers give up nothing—unless their money and their minds count. Well, maybe broccoli; and, occasionally, breakfast as they worshipped Bacchus, the god of hangovers. Meanwhile, admitting I had no life, I holed up in our condo and watched *Mating Rituals of the Wildebeest* on *Animal Planet*. Not that I needed cable...it was happening live outside my window.

Howling catcalls between balconies, young hopefuls coaxed coeds, filled with anonymity-inspired courage, to bare their, uh, souls. Forget *Animal Planet*; it was part-*Animal House*, part-*Rear Window*.

I did journey out a couple of times for a walk on the beach, which was like strolling through a giant ashtray. While the wildlife I saw was hardly endangered, they definitely qualified for reckless endangerment. In fact, sporting my Talbot's one-piece tank suit with built-in bra, tummy panel and flab-concealing skirt, I was closer to extinction than they were.

My husband was the only guy holding his stomach in; the others didn't have one...except for the security guards, who happened to be the only other people "of age" on the island with beach memories of Frankie & Annette, *Beach Blanket Bingo*...and *Jaws*.

After five days and nights, my driver's license picture looked like Glamour Shots compared to what I saw in the mirror.

As Mr. & Mrs. Last Resort crawled home, we were kind of sad knowing that this would probably be our last senior spring break with our son.

Ever-so-thankful for all the stories he never told us, I was particularly grateful for not hearing even those three little words...

"Somebody call forensic."

Life's Obsession

As I lay on our porch one summer reading *The Lovely Bones*, a beautifully written story told through the eyes of a 14-year-old girl in heaven, my daughter commented, "You're obsessed with death."

"Am not."

"Are to."

One of our more heartwarming exchanges.

Does she think this because she sees me reading the obituaries each morning while choking down my daily dose of bran? Or is it because I told her about a dream I had about a near-death experience? How, when I looked back down at my body, I was furious no one had told me how bad my roots were.

Is it because I am transfixed with *Six Feet Under* reruns? Or could it be the Classified Ad pinned to my bulletin board?

USED TOMBSTONE, perfect for anyone named
Homer HendelBergenHeinzel. One only.

I post it neither at poor Homer's expense nor because I intend to buy it (I've already ordered my headstone: I told you I was sick), but because I love how, even facing life's ultimate certainty, there's still room for laughter.

Maybe it's because I volunteer for terminally ill children, take meals to those enduring chemotherapy, or rush to a friend's side who cannot find the right words for her parent's eulogy.

Maybe it's because each time my daughter pulled out of the driveway, was late, or didn't call at the appointed minute, I lunged at her on her return, the mix of love and fear having catapulted me into imagining the worst-case scenario.

Could my daughter know that I wander through Arlington National Cemetery when I visit Washington, D.C.? Has she seen me lingering at the cemetery in my hometown where my father has lain for over 25 years? Seeking a unique comfort—a mix of sorrow and inspiration. It's a small gesture of honor... for I know he is not there.

Perhaps my daughter thinks my alleged obsession is due to our family's inordinate exposure to death lately. With each personal loss I turn inward, seeking to touch the depth of the void, hoping to surface with renewed faith and words of comfort, for renewed faith and words are all I have to use as a momentary salve.

Or maybe it's because I was determined to bear witness to Ground Zero.

By the time I reached Ground Zero, several months after that tragic day, the cleanup was only weeks from being completed. It was hard to visualize two 100+ storied buildings and five others rising from the enormous abyss. The sun, once blocked by the towers' grandeur, shone through, warming those of us who stood frozen on the unfinished wood viewing stands—the sharp-edged grief, although numbed with time, still radiating deep within. The panic and fear we thought had dulled, spiked, causing silent pulses to race once again.

I read many of the biographical sketches in *The New York Times*, each paragraph a masterfully written portrait, a flash illuminating a snapshot of their soul; a splash of color highlighting that special something that made each being unique and cherished.

We've peeled away hundreds of pages from the calendar since then, finding comfort in the buffer of time, yet hoping time won't dull our senses or minimize the importance of the changes we vowed to make.

My daughter would be certain she is correct were she to see me each year on September 11th when I absorb myself in round-the-clock memorials, commentaries and documentaries, reliving that dreaded, late-summer day, terror's shadow cast once again over the steel-blue sky...burning tears returning to still-disbelieving eyes.

But she'd be wrong.

In observance is remembrance. And in remembrance, as we entangle the past with the present, is allegiance to keep their spirit burning bright. Their spirit of pride, of honor, of hope.

No, it's not death with which I am obsessed.

It's life.

As It Should Be

Rarely, do I feel old. There's the stiff back, blurred vision and shrunken calf muscles as brittle as old rubber bands. But after creaking down the stairs for my grande nonfat latte with one Splenda, internally I feel the way I always feel— younger than I am.

But one phone call last fall bolted me upright, in an "S" sort of way. A lifelong friend called to say her daughter was engaged. This child whom I'd known all of her 22 years was getting married.

While she is not my child, without notice, I had gained membership into the M.O.B. (Mother of the Bride) generation—Aunt Bee look-alikes wearing hats, orthotic hose and stale perfume who, sitting within the ribbons, cry into lace hankies.

How could this be? How can our children be getting married when I'm still writing thank-you notes from my wedding? Wasn't it last week I picked out my Engelbert Humperdinck, wide-lapelled, burgundy-velvet going-away pantsuit? My pink high-necked, empire-waisted bridesmaid dresses? My Lenox "Autumn" china, Harvest Gold Crock-Pot and Kromex relish tray? Hadn't I, the one who'd spent her entire life with no middle initial, just monogrammed everything from my toothbrush to the dog bowl to the toilet seat cover?

Sitting within the ribbons at this wedding, my friends and I were in awe. We never looked as sophisticated or worldly as these bridesmaids. They had flawless, glowing skin. They wore sexy dresses with nothing underneath. What's gravity, when you're 22? They had careers. And we, the F.O.M.O.B. (friends of), sat with bone-in busts, forgiving waists, long sleeves...and hobbies.

When I was a bridesmaid, I was interested only in what made up the bride's trousseau. As an F.O.M.O.B., I am interested only in what makes up the bridegroom: his college transcript, benefits and teeth.

More than being thrust into this new position in life, I am caught in the crossroads of time. Just six days earlier, a high school classmate, a man I love as a brother, gently placed his infant son into my arms as I vowed to be the baby's godmother. The day after that, a friend spoke with eloquence and signature irreverence at her mother's funeral.

A wedding. A christening. A funeral.

Old enough for an AARP card, but too young for senior discounts on Lu Ann platters, I watch friends adjust to new permutations of their families. Chairs and high chairs are added to some tables. At others, glasses are raised to the now-empty chair at the head of the table.

I am in the center watching the circle of life; rings of celebration ripple around me.

Within concentric circles, midlife metamorphoses abound: trade-ins on careers, cars and spouses, battles over cancer and custody, face-lifts, stock drops, religious rebirths, stagnant stability. As the wheel of fortune turns, some will sail through troubles and soar to the stars. And some will stumble and get lost in their misfortune.

Although I'm almost 30 years older than the newlyweds and would have to be strapped to an IV dispensing bags of B-12 and Prozac to tackle motherhood again, I don't necessarily embrace adding years to my bottom line. Some days, though, I think, if I were in charge, I might trade my stiff back, blurred vision and shrunken calf muscles for youth with its glowing skin, sexy dresses, and a real career.

Thank God, I'm not in charge.

So I smile with secret pleasure in being where I am, past my salad days, maybe even scooping up the last forkful of the main course. But, with the promise of dessert around the corner, I am able, at last, to laugh at funerals and cry at christenings and weddings. And I wouldn't give back one year of life I've lived.

And, that, I think, is as it should be.

Stir It Up

I've seen that look before. The facial tic, the grinding molars, the gnawing the table leg—we need a vacation.

"Let's grab the kids and go...anywhere. It'll be great," my husband said.

Unfortunately, my days of spontaneity died with my last college road trip when we left for Mexico at midnight, barely making it back in time for our 8 o'clock class...the next semester.

But a trip is usually a great idea...maybe even do-able with the help of some fine pharmaceuticals. Nothing makes me crazier than trying to leave town. Like Captain Queeg and those strawberries, I lose it trying to tackle everything I've put off since the Reagan era. I buy wedding presents for couples that now have three children; bake a cake for the couple who moved next door...in 1979; and buy new underwear for the entire family, in case we have a wreck.

Once I actually get out of town, I loosen up. When I took my son to college orientation in Virginia the summer after his high school graduation, we went to one seminar...and bolted.

Forget scheduling his first-year classes, we were on the same longitude as the Baltimore Orioles. "Mom, it's only a three-hour drive." Too bad we had a nine o'clock flight home the next morning.

"Mom, it's *Camden Yards*."

All right, then.

Heading north in our rented Hyundai, we wrestled D.C.'s 18 beltways with five lanes of traffic moving anywhere from reverse to 300 miles per hour. I lost count how many illegal U-turns we took.

My son, panicked that we would miss one note of *The Star-Spangled Banner*, floored it. Just my luck, we got there in time for batting practice. Even better luck—the game went into extra innings! Extra innings for me is like the ballet performing extra *pas de deux's* for my son.

In the 11th inning, we moved from our seats in the nose-bleed section to behind home plate where we had our pick of ten rows of empty box seats. We enjoyed at least one pitch before the Eva Braun of ballpark ushers asked to see our tickets. I was mortified—a mother, son in tow, sneaking into seats illegally.

My son, lying to Eva, said our real seats were actually only two rows back—which is where she banished us for the rest of the game. Hate that. As I watched other felonious seat-moochers try to capture Eva's Western Front, the game went on...and on...and...

The 14th-inning stretch reminded me of the Astros/Mets

playoff game in 1986—the one that ended in 1987.

The game was over at 12:30—as in morning. Blurry-eyed, I hit I-95 North, which made the return trip interesting since Virginia is to the South.

The extra hours were filled with my son passionately and painstakingly reviewing the greatest music era ever—mine. I listened to thousands of verses of Bob Marley as my son lectured on Rastafarianism, which, apparently, is a religion. I thought it was a hairdo.

At 3:30 a.m. (I hadn't seen 3:30 a.m. since the last time I set my alarm for pain medication), we rolled into what my son called a ghetto Bates Motel. "Norman" gave us his last room—smoking, of course.

After sleeping all of four hours in the world's largest ashtray, I awoke to find I, indeed, looked like a Rastafarian—the hairdo—and smelled like a Ganja worshipper.

Unimpressed with our vagabond looks, airport security completely overlooked us, thank goodness. They were too busy mauling the 80-something little old lady in support hose with the suspicious-looking walker.

I'm not saying this trip aged me, but my next spur-of-the-moment road trip will probably be in the back of a hearse. But for one night, my son and I, as Bob Marley would say, we "stir it up, mon."

It was an adventure I wouldn't have traded for all the innings in the world.

Not there possibly could have been any more.

The More Things Change...

On our way to kindergarten, anxiety filled the car. "Don't be frightened," I said. "School's an adventure—you'll make new friends, learn cool stuff and eat in a cafeteria. When school's out, I'll be waiting for you. You're a big boy now."

What I didn't say was, *Will you find your way without me? Will you be kind, share, and pick up after yourself? The days are my own now...but how will I fill them? It will never be the same.*

His big, brown eyes widened with fears unspoken. *I don't want to go to this big school. What if I don't make any friends? What if I'm the dumbest one here? What if everyone else knows what to do and I don't? Why can't I stay home? Will you forget me? Why do things have to change?*

But all he said was, "Don't kiss me goodbye in front of the kids."

Wasn't that just a few days ago? And now,college.

As I drove him and his older, more experienced sister to Virginia, my son, trying to envision his new life, was audibly silent.

For 1200 miles, our senses were heightened as we barreled through state after state. My daughter peered through the windshield, looking ahead, anxious to resume the life she'd so carefully created her freshman year...one of independence, the only umbilical cord remaining tied now is to our credit. My son stared wistfully out of the rear window, looking back—on his old life, his friends, his dog, his car—wrapping himself in the comfort of the way things were.

Looking neither forward nor backward, I simply wanted time to stand still—hoping that somewhere in the stillness I'd find comfort in this juncture...and make sense of how it happened so quickly.

"How long will it take me to adjust?" he asked. How long, I wondered, for us all?

Swaying behind us was the U-Haul bearing their worldly belongings; its motto, *reisaE edaM gnivoM,* consuming the rearview mirror. If this is easy, I thought, I'll never survive hard. During some of the miles when my daughter was driving, I was scrunched down in the back seat, I listened to Dave Matthews and the drone of the tires on the pavement, savoring the sound of their voices.

"You know college is an adventure," I interjected. "You'll make new friends, take cool classes and eat cold pizza for breakfast. But clean underwear doesn't reproduce itself, you know. And I hope you packed an alarm clock that can wake the dead."

What I didn't say was, *When school's out, I'll be waiting for you. You're a man now. It's time to find your way on your own. Will you remember to share, be kind, and pick up after yourself? The days are my own now...but how will I fill them? It will never be the same.*

When we arrived on campus, his fears remained locked in his throat. *I don't want to go to this big school. What if I don't make any friends? What if I'm the dumbest one here? What if everyone else knows what to do and I don't? Why can't I stay home? Will everyone forget me? Why do things have to change?*

But all he said was, "Later."

At home, inside two empty rooms down the hall, the beds remain made, the towels off the floor and the CD player silent. With the days my own, my grocery list consists of support hose, Diet Coke and Gingkoba. My schedule's reduced now to one child; too young to date, too old for babysitters, she's filled with the promise to keep us young.

The phone rings. "Mom," he says, "can't talk, but...it's awesome."

And the next chapter begins.

A Socko Finish

The voice on the phone sounded near death, "Mom, bad news." Which in itself is an unremarkable and verifiable truth. "I've been assassinated."

Naturally, I was devastated. And particularly shocked to hear it from the victim himself. I'd certainly seen him in varying states in which he could've been mistaken for dead—as, I'm sure, had his professors—but the finality.

Unfortunately, there'd be no floral arrangements. And no fat check from that goose at AFLAC.

"It's the game, remember?" my husband said.

Oh, yeah, the game. The freshman game in which 100 stormin' dorm-men playing neophyte hit-men knock each other off...with a wadded-up sock. God knows, in an institution of higher education, those are certainly plentiful.

"The mental strain is unbelievable," my son said, fatigued, in his weekly updates. Silly, I thought the mental strain might come from lectures, papers, finals. "I'm constantly watching my back while planning my own hit."

If his IQ dropped much lower, I suggested he sell.

This death-at-all-costs game turning strangers into targets was, duh, really about money...a kitty of $150. A victim couldn't be bumped off if he/she was in his/her room, classroom or the bathroom. For the Happy Hunting zones, they had "safeties"—instruments of defense created each week by the Dorm House Council, which is like the CIA, but with more aliases and fake IDs.

The first safety was a Band-Aid on the face. This essentially eliminated most of the girls who were playing because they feared that, ewww gross, it'd look like they were covering up a zit.

Next was the Rally Cap plus—and this is a real brain-tickler—a pen behind the ear. This definitely separated those with ADD. from those who can't spell ADD.

Other safeties included wearing your clothes inside out (as if that made any day different), a pillow under your shirt, a banana around your neck, CDs taped to the back of both hands and other unmentionables that I wouldn't describe in detail anywhere but at Rick's XXXX Bookstore.

Parents Weekend was particularly heartwarming as I walked across grounds with my son wearing a towel turban on his head...secured with bobby pins. I didn't know whether to be more concerned that he had bobby pins...or that he knew how to use them. Soon, the bobby pins were replaced with his secret weapon: duct tape.

He looked like a homeless Carmen Miranda.

The final safety—a real piece of resistance—everywhere he went, he had to carry...his box fan.

Imagine lobbying your professor for a C-...holding a box fan. Mantle-diving with...a box fan. At the Corner at 2:30 a.m., eating a one-eyed-bacon-double-cheeseburger (because you can) sitting with...a box fan. Tiring easily, he dragged out a roll of duct tape and, fashioning his roommate's now-shredded Ralph Lauren bath towel as straps, he made his box fan into a backpack.

What a resume builder.

Down to two finalists, all safeties were declared null and void. It was open hunting season. Spies, easily recruited with Skittles and MD 20/20, ratted on my son's location. Walking out of his friend's room...he was socked.

Unfortunately, it wasn't a painless death. After thirteen weeks of mental warfare and strategizing, the end was insufferable. He walked away with the same amount of money as those who'd been eliminated the first week—zip, zero, nada.

I knew that, as a student at a university rich in history and tradition, he would be exposed to rituals reaching back to its founding in the early 1800s. Just as I knew that, after the rigorous selection process, if he was admitted, he would pass. Silly me, I was thinking "pass," as in grades.

Needing closure, I penned his obituary:

Four-square enthusiast, Parsley, was socked today after battling for his life trapped inside his dorm room with only an empty Gatorade bottle and 987 Bob Marley CDs. He will best be remembered for being a game player, his unruly hair and retro Oilers jacket. While his IQ indicated that he was nothing shy of a full six-pack, his actions indicated he lacked the plastic thing that held it together. He is survived by his mother, noted Angelina Jolie look-alike.

The Point, After All

Dateline: Two dirty bombs went off today in bedrooms on the second floor of a nearby home. Unsuspecting residents, in recovery from visiting college children, report they never heard a thing. Hysterical deafness apparently set in soon after the family was reunited.

Reported casualties: discarded Christmas presents; unstamped thankyou notes from 1991; shredded napkins with names and cell phone numbers scrawled in hieroglyphics; and melted CDs from being burned at warp speed.

Missing in action: the children's inheritance.

Isn't it enough that we've sold our internal organs to pay for these kids to go away to college? Must they keep coming home?

Ever since their return, we've been under red terror alert: immobilized as we listen to them rail against our conservatism, capitalism, and materialism—just before they ask where they'll be sitting at the Super Bowl.

I am paralyzed with fear of saying the wrong thing—
"Ah, up at the crack of dusk already?" I am held hostage as
they take my car, leaving theirs...with the nail-punctured tires,
expired inspection stickers and warrants for their arrest.

Left on our own to forage for food, we find only their petrified chili con queso and concrete pizza. No wonder we're
deaf—our arteries are so clogged, our ear canals are blocked.

It's like having newborns again; getting up every half-
hour and looking for their bottles. Even our conversations are
like déjà vu.

2:30 a.m.

"Did you hear something?"

"Yes. Heavy breathing...and the dog sounding like he's
about to throw up."

"We don't have a dog. That was you."

3:45 a.m. (Sound of car crashing into the dining room.)

"There, hear that? That has to be them."

"Can't be. They just called to say they're hitting a drive-
thru and coming home."

"Simultaneously?"

4:30 a.m.

"Do you know where your children are?"

"Where they are? I don't even know who they are."

"Well, they were your idea. I'd have been happy with a
mute parakeet."

"Shh, I hear elephants on the stairs. Pretend you're asleep
and maybe they'll go away."

"You've been saying that for 21 years."

Getting kids to this point of independence, as I recall, was the
point, after all. Although tempted to stop when the labor nurse
advised me to, I didn't. In fact, I'd just begun—pushing them to
think outside the box, be their own person, find their passion.

By my daughter's junior year—freshly legal at age 21 years, 2
days, 45 minutes—there was, at last, a glimmer of maturity—even

a bit of role reversal—in this verbal exchange:

"I can't believe you got to the Becks' bay house and didn't call me!" she hollers ten counties away.

I stared into the phone. Me? Call her? When I, huh? "Well, um, sorry. Yeah, I'm okay."

"You're okay? Who cares?"

"Wait. I thought you just said, 'I can't believe you got to the Becks' bay house and didn't call me'?"

"Are you deaf? I said, 'I can't believe I went to Spec's Liquor Warehouse and they didn't card me!'"

Back to reality, I stand once again at the threshold to their rooms. The destruction and contamination left from their dirty bombs rival what lurks behind my refrigerator. I close their doors, secure that, unless they're hiding under the mounds of debris, they're gone. Back to their worlds—where learning about the world is their job. A job with no hours, no maid service and unlimited cell phone minutes after 7 p.m.—in perfect sync with the time they get up.

Exhausted, I find solace between my covers. I have my life back.

Or do I?

That Boy, I Swear...

For twenty years, it's been a fine line we've walked. Somewhere between wondering what alien beings delivered him to us—and being so much alike that before he even opens his mouth, I feel the flames fueling his passion as my own.

We lived through the pre-school temper tantrums; he, in his cowboy boots and flattened Stetson, ever-armed with his

Ninja Turtle Nunchucks. We survived the "it's-not-my-fault" preteens and lived through his adolescence on a-need-to-know basis. We outlived the never-ending "When am I going to grow?" proving, at last, that genes and faith go the distance... for him, past six feet.

We even weathered the lines drawn in the sand, usually long after the hour hand swept past the wee numbers. Each side stabbing at complete conquest, true victory was hidden in the folds of hearing, understanding one another just a fraction more.

After each cajoling, each hug, tear, and giggle, I'd smile gratefully, "That boy, I swear..."

During our Hill Country summers when he was small, after the lightning bugs were secured, we'd let the night fall over us, watching the darkness pull the moon to the top of the sky. His small hand would point to a brilliant cluster. "If I could, I'd give you those stars, Mom."

And now, in a twinkle, that boy, I swear, he's all grown up.

With his dad, the great equalizer through it all has been the Big 12, ACC, Final Four...the Series. Many nights I've been lulled to sleep by their voices rehashing the day's standings, double plays and slam dunks. Their familiar cadence and soft drawls punctuated with animation, wrapped in consummate contentment. Even when the air was thick and harsh between them and they couldn't find the words, there was always, "How 'bout that draft...?"

Their bonding force...their tie that binds.

When a certain wildly extravagant opportunity arose recently, I jumped at it. Two tickets to the Super Bowl, one with my husband's name on it. The other...

"Mom," he said, "I can't. It's too much. I'll get to a Super Bowl someday..."

"But not with your father," I replied softly.

Catching a red-eye flight from college, the boy slipped

home, undetected. Exchanging phone calls all day, his dad thought there were ten states between them as they talked three times.

"Did you see Billet's three-pointer?"

"And that technical..."

On our way to dinner, the cell phone rang again, abruptly halting his dad's steps in the parking lot. As his shoulders softened and that smile fell across his face...I knew he was listening to more stats.

As their conversation closed, hindsight prompting more than half-wishes his boy could be with him for the game, he asked, "What are you doing for the Super Bowl—big party?"

Static crept over the line. Thinking perhaps they'd been disconnected, he was cognizant briefly that he hadn't squeezed in his customary "I love you, son" before pressing "End."

From nowhere, a hand squeezed his shoulder. He turned, expecting an unannounced friend.

More than a friend, it was a familiar silhouette, one he knew better than his own. One whose shadow only recently had overtaken his own.

The boy, standing eye-to-eye, his cell phone to his ear, talked on, "No, Dad, the Super Bowl...I'm sitting with you."

Eerily, this boy has managed to combine his father's love of sports with mine of writing. Hitting deadlines as the sports editor of his college newspaper is not all at which he excels.

The day after the game, under his byline read "...the best game ever—but being next to the person who planted inside of me my love of sports made it the best day of my life."

Days later, I received a handwritten note with his signature scrawling, "You made my wish a reality." In these words, I sensed a familiar cadence, his soft drawl wrapped in consummate contentment.

A boy no longer. I smile gratefully, "That man, I swear..."

Letting Go

Eloise's Commencement

As a little girl, I dreamed of being a ballerina, an astronaut and marrying Zorro. I dreamed of this in the silence of my room, sent there for acting like Eloise...if only I'd had the room service, the charge account and the Plaza Hotel.

As a college student, I dreamed of feeding the hungry, learning to skydive and being Katharine Hepburn. I dreamed of this silently while reading Kierkegaard, seeking the perfect tan and watching *I Love Lucy*.

As a wife and mother, I dream of being better at each, hitting the floor on my knees every day, asking for strength to allow it to happen. Impatiently, I wait.

But in the silent, unannounced moments, I trace the outlines of clouds taking shape in my mind and dream of young people... like myself. And, I wonder, what do their dreams hold?

Striking my best Eloise pose, I pour make-believe tea and give my commencement address to my imaginary graduating class:

First, I ask you to please turn on your cell phones—you might welcome the interruption.

Now, please lay down your mental backpacks filled with future burdens. In this small window of time, there are no papers due, no peer pressures, no parental demands, no masks of imitation. Just be still...the only sound, your own heart beating. It's your turn now—to get down to the business of being you.

You are an overscheduled lot, raised in the backseat of a car between soccer, science camp and SAT prep. Rigorous schedules packed with our good intent—to make you a better person, better than any other generation, to give you an edge. But over what?

Part parent/part human beings, we made mistakes out of fear and love, blurring what we thought was right for you... with what is right for you, pushing and pulling you along the path to greatness. Our path to greatness.

It's time now for you to step off the treadmill and uncover the real you, find your purpose.

You have been trained to see yourself in a grade, a trophy, a paycheck or the warmth of another—and may have overlooked the face in the mirror. What you seek is there. I have seen it in your eyes, a reflection of your heart and mind. But you must get still enough to listen to the silent things on the other side of the everyday world that only you can hear...in your own heart.

That is where success resides.

Uncovering your purpose, you will find the arms that will catch you when you fall, get a bad lab report, or lose a loved one. And the hands that will guide the way to the great job, the loving soul mate, a life well-lived.

Find something larger than yourself. Embrace your own mortality. Be generous. Highlight the humor. And get to know us, your parents. We're smarter than when you last knew us, getting smarter every day...but our days together grow fewer.

Sometimes it takes a long time to be the person you want to be. I tried on many lives before finding my own. I still act, at times, like Eloise, a closet kid in an aging body. I know now I could never be Katharine Hepburn—there was only one. But I still long to feed the hungry, skydive and be a most awesome mother. It's not too late.

So, each day I get down to the business of being me. There is only one. And most days I find her, in the stillness, that face in my mirror.

"It is never too late to be what you might have been," wrote George Eliot. I have been thinking...it is never too early, either.

Letting Go

Seedlings and Snapshots

They'd lived a full life, their age-old roots sinking deep beneath their green-grass apron. After 100 years—their once-dense structures, no longer able to sustain their massive trunks and towering limbs, gave way—four majestic oaks toppled to the ground like slain giants.

For the lifetime of summers I've come to this place, summers strung together like trotlines along the riverbank below, those trees stood tall as sentries, providing shade as the sun rose over the hill, spilling its light onto the porch as we slept.

Peering across the deeply empty space where the old oaks once stood, their remnants stacked neatly now on the side of the property, I try to imagine how long it will take for the newly-planted seedlings to replace them. But the new trees are not for me to see grow into themselves...rather for three children.

Inside the glassed-in sleeping porch, the sun pours in unfiltered as I tackle my annual task—sorting photographs into albums. Hundreds of images scattered across the table will make their way into their own home—the album of family trips, the Christmas album, the wordless narrative of each child's life. If not for these prints, I doubt I could remember so readily the soft, dark curls framing enormous chestnut-brown eyes, her lower lip, half-bitten, forming a small pouch. Or the passionate warrior-tyke dressed daily in cowboy boots, hat and shorts, ever-armed with a toy gun, baseball bat or a look that could kill. And the youngest with gold-brown ringlets, whose peering eyes, mega-watt smile and soft laugh said she was happy each day just to be here...and made me wonder where she came from.

These albums tell their stories—the good parts of their stories. Left lingering in the backs of their minds is the mind-numbing routine—constant goading to do homework, torturous dinners, their vegetables staring at them, and tempers lost over spilled milk. These books illustrate the heart-to-hearts—the heart-to-hearts that, hopefully, will rise above the routine, impressing upon their souls each fulfilling moment, each achievement, each tradition...each memory.

In their own separate manner, each child would pull from the shelves in my bedroom one volume that spoke to them at that given moment. Sprawled on the floor alongside my bed, they'd lie for hours on their stomachs, ankles crossed, heads held in the palm of one hand, flipping the pages of their young lives. They'd float, lifted as if rafting down the river 107 steps below me, carried by a current of life events that define them. And, silently, I'd wonder—perhaps they wondered, too—what future volumes might hold.

Consumed with looking at their own faces in the pictures of their glory days, the kids wouldn't give a second look at the parent alongside them. They were wholly uninterested in pursuing that which is impossible—knowing the side of us that wasn't labeled "mom and dad." As toddlers, they saw us only as guides; as teens, special prosecutors; as young adults, their Supreme Court sitting in judgment.

I wonder if they saw our love, concern and pride? Or is that reserved for a later time? When they feel the touch of their own child's hand, demand they eat their vegetables or, standing on the sidelines, cannot focus their camera through their own tears—maybe then they will come to know the other side of us.

As I chronicle their lives, time stands still. I look out at the new trees taking root in the footprints of the giants that went before them, each full of hope. A work of the ages, a labor of love, laying the groundwork for ensuing generations is a job most fulfilling...building the stories of us, the stories of them.

Flashes of moments captured in perpetuity, rooted in the past.

Letting Go

Still Here, After All These Years

D ear parents of graduating high school seniors:
It will be okay. Remember, this was the plan all along.

The only thing between you and saying goodbye to that nocturnal carnivore down the hall is the longest summer of your life. It's not easy sharing airspace with someone filled with such bottomless intelligence, independence...and need for money.

But come the first day of college, your freshman will reside, along with every other freshman, at the bottom of the food chain, feeling as if they know nothing.

At last, something on which you can agree.

No longer will you hear his high school mantra: "It's not my fault." In fact, you won't hear anything because you will have been put on, without notice, a need-to-know basis. In part, thanks to caller ID. And once he's convinced you to transfer $384,797 into his banking account for poker losses sustained to upperclassmen, there's nothing left to say.

Her freshman year, you will wish late-night phone calls were as simple as "I ran out of gas." So far, the calls I've received from my son and daughter, now in their third and fourth year (notice I didn't say junior and senior), have ranged from: "Have the campus police called you, yet?" to "What's our deductible?" to "What in the heck is cream of tartar and why isn't it in the dairy section?!"

There will be those rare, poignant occasions when she will turn to you for meaningful, soulful conversations...in tears: the nympho/klepto/pyscho roommate, the moron advisor who recommended 8 a.m. classes; the idiot professor that assigns, of all things, papers. Or perhaps it will be good news: he traded his bed for a hammock and computer for a blender...for a more tropical feel in the dorm room.

You'll hang up and go to bed for four days, asking God where you went wrong. And your freshman will go out...and wins the Beer Pong Championship.

By Thanksgiving, after he has charged $179 to the airline in overweight charges (dirty clothes), you'll realize you've adjusted to his absence. By Christmas, he will appear older... and wider. Not solely because he's been strapping on the Midnight feedbag, but because he won't waste their time or your money on Low Carb/Light beer.

My father's advice to my brother when he left for college was, "Take accounting." As an aside, Dad also cautioned him to "beware of girls with twigs in their beak—they might be looking to nest."

His advice to me was: "Don't drink anything out of a garbage can." You might consider giving your freshman all three. But most of your children will turn to wiser, more seasoned sophomores for the real skinny: "Don't put hot dogs in toasters." "If you find a hair in your food in the dining hall, just assume it's yours and move on." "Beware when buying used books. The person who had the highlighter before may have been an idiot." When asked what to bring from home, beer helmet, shower sandals and underwear rank among the top three with sophomores.

Parents, whether it's your first child to go to college or your last, whether you're facing an empty nest or just an empty bed, it's far tougher than you'll ever imagine. You can take spur-of-the-moment vacations and not alert the police to possible conventions convening at your home at 2 a.m. You'll actually get to sleep through the night, blissfully ignorant of where your child is, nor caring.

But, you'll have to reintroduce yourself to your spouse, discussing things other than homework, exams, and detention schedules. Looking this person in the eye with whom you've been living for what feels like several lifetimes, you'll ask probing questions such as, "What's your name again?"

And when you visit your child at college the first time,

taking his entire dorm out for Surf 'N Turf platters and Baked Alaska, you'll phone him Sunday afternoon before returning home. At last, he will answer groggily and mumble, "You're still here?"

And you'll think...that's the plan. Forever.

Path of Most Resistance

Having just bid goodbye to my son as he makes his way back to school, I can't think of anything that lasts longer than college Christmas break. Maybe Cher's farewell tour.

On Day One, it felt like he'd been here an eternity...and he hadn't even arrived home. The first step of the marathon was a phone call from his driveway at school, "What did you do with the spare key to my car?"

Having been down similar roads with him before, each adding another layer of tire tracks down my back, I knew there was no point in asking the obvious, "Why?"

He was in the state of Virginia. His keys were in his friend's pocket...on their way to the state of North Carolina. Knowing my son had a plane to catch to Jamaica the next day—from the state of Maryland—I fell into a state of depression.

The only certainty in the uncertain life of a 21-year-old boy-to-man is that, within hours, Problem Number One will take a back seat to new-and-improved Problem Number Two. It's the triage of parenting.

Near midnight, our phone rang. "My-best-friend-said-I-could-take-his-car-to-the-airport-tomorrow-so-yeah-it's-a-stickshift-and-no-I've-never-driven-one-so-I-was-practicing-but-it's-icy-and-snowing-and-I-slid-down-this-hill-into-some-mean-guy's-yard-and-I'm-stuck-so-like-who-do-I-call-to-get-towed?"

Pouring myself a couple of shots, I let my fingers do the walking, past AA, to Triple AAA. "Chill, mom," he said, listening to my teeth grind. It has taken years, but finally I understand the meaning of his compassion-packed command: "This, too, shall pass."

And it did. But only to make room for Problem Number Three.

The next morning, sitting in, of all things, a funeral, my phone vibrated with a text message. "Missed my plane. Why didn't you tell me I needed my passport to leave the country?" I'd never envied the deceased more.

After Christmas, came his ski trip. And more calls: "I lost my cell phone." "I lost my shoes." "My elbow bends 90 degrees—the wrong way." "My nose hemorrhaged." "My flight was cancelled."

I don't know what I was doing when I thought I was teaching him survival skills, but if I had a guardian angel of motherhood, she must have stepped out...to chain-smoke.

Having enjoyed a full-term childhood, my son, not liking change, is reticent to shed it. Something I should've known when, from ages 2 to 9, he'd only wear his red-print, dinosaur shorts, cowboy boots and threadbare blue T-shirt permanently stained with cherry Kool-Aid. He looked like a walking victim of a drive-by shooting.

Now listening to Bob Marley to the point of making our hair hurt, he only wears clothes from Value Village, a landfill that sells massively-used clothes...by the pound. On formal occasions, he wears his grandfather's herringbone jacket. And in a certain Bob Marley phase (nine years and counting), he's looked like he swallowed a St. Bernard, whose tail is sticking out.

While he doesn't know how much things cost and doesn't care, he absorbs ideas, knowledge and people like a giant sponge. Over time, he's come to offer a firm handshake to adults and freely hug his grandmother, and his arguments have evolved from what he's against...to what he's for.

Maybe I didn't do exactly a bang-up job raising him to be independent. Maybe it was easier for me to step in and do things for him. Or maybe, deep down, I knew that the list of things I could do for him would slowly dwindle, and I would go from being his first source...to his last resort.

Somewhere in the midst of losing things, forgetting things and breaking things, he picked up survival skills of another kind. In a note he left his little sister before going back to school, he wrote, "Don't underestimate Bob Marley. It's not just his music, it's his message: love, respect, righteousness, faith, kindness and humbleness. Live this and live fulfilled."

Like his grandfather's herringbone jacket, full-blown maturity is still something he's trying on. While the jacket hangs slightly baggy now, someday, I suspect, it will be a perfect fit.

A Minors Offense

Maybe I should follow my kids' advice—Get a life. Others probably agree. Others being those populating the neighboring Little League fields that I stalk on spring evenings, searching for the past...and a side of barbeque, extra jalapenos, please.

Long past our son's Little League glory days, I miss the ancient spring ritual of breaking in his newly-assigned cap— backing the car over it, grinding dirt into its seams and soaking its rubber-banded bill in a glass of water, praying filthy, frayed edges and an upside down "U" framing his face would make him an All-Star.

Yet, I'm still drawn to the fields—a good place to go to savor life.

By self-invitation, I flew to another field eight states away where the sights, sounds and smells revive memories. Green-pea wannabes fresh from a win—or loss—racing for a snow cone; angst-filled parents twitching in the stands; and the freshly mown grass, watered down baselines and kids' sweat equity filling the air with the smell of old pennies.

Wafting up from the Minors field was a familiar whine...a green pea at third base. Confronting six different coaches, the whine bellowed, "Stop *yelling* at me!"

There, stood a familiar silhouette—a filthy-, frayed-capped baseball worshipper watching the batter intently, anticipating the next play...and the next...just as he'd done 11 years ago. The little boy I'd watched play catch by himself for hours in our backyard stood not on third base, but to the left...as coach.

Reminiscent of the *Bad News Bears*, the team sponsor was not Chico's Bail Bonds, but Dixie Pawn. The team going by the name "Pawns." The coaching staff, a lineup of usual suspects, had each assumed their hero's identity. Duct-taped onto their 99-cent T-shirts were Dusty Baker, Larry Bowa, Bobby Cox, Dave Duncan, Don Zimmer, managed by our son, Lou Piniella. Slaves, but not to fashion—in black Converse lowtops and lower-slung pants (any lower and I'd be posting bail)—they lacked only a cardboard sign: "Will coach for beer."

Sitting in the dugout (one perk to birthing the coach), I met Hunter, the catcher, and Quinn, a.k.a. Dontrelle Willis, each focused on how far they could spit their sunflower seeds. "Who are you?" Hunter asked, reloading his dimpled cheeks with ammo.

"Coach Piniella's mother." Hunter eyed me with the same disbelief he would a black-and-white TV from the pre-

Columbian era. He'd heard of them, but never seen one.

"How 'bout these coaches?" I asked.

Screwing up his freckled nose, he said, "I guess we're lucky to have...most of 'em." We talked about his third-grade teacher who's pretty cool, his dog that sleeps with him who's very cool, and his second game ever—this one. "Why are you taking notes?" he asked.

"I'm a writer."

"For *Sports Illustrated*?" he whooped, then spelled his last name, slowly, respectful of accuracy...and my pre-Columbian mummyhood.

Meanwhile, my husband—whom the Pawns figured could've been, to quote Lasorda, a waiter at the Last Supper—was backseat coaching. "Move your 3rd baseman to 1st!" "Swing up!" "Glove to the ground, boys!" Ducking sunflower seeds shooting past with AK47 repetition, I sat silently. Mrs. Piniella never would've hollered at the Mariners.

Back home on Sunday evenings, I now await Coach's post-game wrap-up—Quinn's homers, Hunter's uncatchable catches and, of course, the good-looking moms. In his voice shines the true highlight: six college buddies stepping up to the plate, taking time out to relive and recycle their childhood love...from the other side.

In the twilight, they take another turn at bat, playing their hearts out as the boys they will always be. A fight to the finish...home run derby. And the crowd goes wild...

Another season for the books—another chapter of one fine life.

Who Knew?

Sometime after panty raids but before laptops, studying abroad became as essential to college life as fake IDs. The kids argue, of course, that it's about broadening horizons, experiencing other cultures and learning to be on their own. Spending five months in a fabulous foreign country where Cokes cost $8.00, all cars are stick shifts, and Starbucks appear only on every other corner is now construed as "roughing it."

But all this really means is that after they graduate and come back home to live—worldly and widely unemployable—they can then turn to their parents and say, "Whaddya mean, I have to pay my own cell phone bill?"

Our first contact with our daughter, who was roughing it in Spain one spring, was an e-mail: "I met a salsa professor." Unfortunately, his last name was not Pace, which could have led to piles of money.

Equally unfortunate, I tried to explain, is that there is no such thing as a salsa professor. And she tried to explain to me, using her pithy and universal throw-down, "Whatever."

Later, I came to appreciate the salsa professor not only for his creativity, but also for the balance he provided...to her future e-mails: The Brazilian race car driver, the drunk Irishman with three teeth who proposed to her, and the dark-haired Spanish bullfighter with clear, green eyes she met on the back of a motorcycle.

Be still, my heart. I recall too well the power of an accent.

She did utter the term "class" once, in conjunction with the verb, "dropped." When I casually asked "So, how's your Spanish coming?" she said, "My phonetics professor was so rude. He expected me to roll my Rs and stuff."

Who knew?

Apparently, this handicap didn't bother Ruben, Roberto or Romeo.

Letting Go

But for one phone call home asking if cell phones are waterproof, most talk centered on her travels—Portugal, Prague, Budapest, Vienna. Vienna, a city, at last, where she contacted a family friend and met up with him.

You can only imagine our glee when he wrote this first-hand account:

"I had the great pleasure of feeding your daughter yesterday.

"Her 'roommate' you mentioned, was nowhere in sight, but Antonio certainly was—he just couldn't keep his hands off of her. With a lot of good old soap and water, some comprehensive dental treatment, clean clothes, a shave and haircut, he could become a marginally presentable—although still annoying—son-in-law. Nonetheless, I'm sure that their plan to marry in Spain and reside in his Volkswagen van is a relief to you financially. You save not only the cost of the wedding, but also that annoying last year of college tuition.

"She appeared to be in good spirits and, for the most part, in good health. I couldn't help but notice her nasty infection secondary to the large 'Antonio' tattoo inked on her left forearm by a street artist in Budapest. But good news! The area immediately surrounding the chrome stud through her right nostril, while still inflamed, was healing somewhat better.

"Antonio's difficulty with some creditors in Spain made their return difficult, so I gave her a check for 15,000 Euros. In repaying me, you can use those now unnecessary tuition funds for next year. That comes to $18,510 at today's exchange rate—that weak dollar, you know.

"Delighted to meet your pride and joy. She's a great one all right."

Mullets that we are, we actually agreed when our son explained why he wanted to study in Geneva—to pursue his interest in international relations.

I was too scared to ask him to define "relations."

When he called to say he was busy analyzing Swiss Miss,

133

I could only dream that he was referring to the company's financial statement.

We heard from him once. "I'm sunbathing on a nude beach in Mallorca..."

Accidentally-on-purpose dropping my cell phone into a sink of soaking dirty dishes, the line went dead. Guess they aren't waterproof after all.

Who knew?

Pumps...and Circumstance

Academic prowess was never my middle name. In fact, it's hard to pinpoint the nadir of my undergrad years. Perhaps it was taking life-altering classes such as "Politics of Love and Altruism," pass/fail, of course; or maybe it was procrastinating until the last day of the semester to map the night sky for my Astronomy final which—and this is ironic—happened to coincide with a torrential downpour.

But, in hindsight, my most nagging non-effort, hands down, was not attending my own college graduation.

It's not that I feared wearing a gown that could double as a four-panel van cover (validating the question, "Does this make me look fat?") or a cap that looks like a flattened pizza box. I no-showed because I was a Poli Sci major and, matriculating at a public university large enough to sponsor its own space program, the diploma ceremony for Poli Sci majors was relegated to the natatorium.

Thinking all 5-syllable words sound alike, I confused natatorium with sanatorium...and ordered a straitjacket. It wasn't until years later that I realized what I really needed were nose clips.

So, no mortarboard for me. Although, I did attend my Bored Martyrs graduation—an illustrious group with impossibly high admission requirements: an insatiable need for beer, a strong bladder...and Dad's credit card.

Last week, I participated in my first real college commencement—my daughter's. Standing amid the throng of tuition underwriters, I listened as "Pomp and Circumstance" played ceaselessly for 73 minutes, my teeth numb by round 19, and watched 1.59 million twenty-somethings process ceremoniously from the University's Rotunda down the Lawn of tradition. Having traded in their *Animal House* togas for togas scholastica, a sea of caps and gowns came in waves—velvet tams, jewel-toned hoods, honor cords, medallions, sunglasses, flip-flops, toe rings, body piercings and hair colors from the underground.

Steeped in tradition, the ceremony was, in the president's words, simultaneously ageless and current. On hallowed grounds, majestic arms of the colonnades welcomed these graduates into its history. Giant ash trees stood as sentries casting purple shadows over the Lawn; it was as if time stood still.

As students paraded down the trampled grass path, dangling from their bodies were the surgically-attached instruments of their generation: cell phones, pagers and iPods. Some appeared to walk on air, almost as giddy as their parents who were spastic with emotion.

Obviously, these kids have accepted job offers.

Others appeared to walk on air, too—from inhaling the helium-filled Tweety Bird balloon attached to their tasseled cap.

The only things surgically attached to my daughter, bringing up the rear, dead-last in the lineup, were her Magnums Cum Laude—empty peach and mango Boone's Farm wine bottles. Apparently, a lesser-known tradition was that the bars open on Commencement Day at 6 a.m.

As the speaker addressed those members of her class

who will make history by curing cancer, eradicating AIDS and overcoming terrorism, I looked across the rows of flattened-pizza-boxes and spotted the bright pink pants peeking out from under my daughter's gown. Laughing affably with her friends-for-life, her eyes sparkled, even from a distance.

Her cheeks flush with color, her body animated with anticipation, she is anxious to begin the life of which she's always dreamed. A life of independence. No longer the little girl torn between becoming a stunt double or helicopter commando, she has real plans now—plans that require a chocolate-brown leather satchel, BlackBerry and a 401K. But first, Cooperstown, skydiving, and traveling the world...by motorcycle.

As caps and balloons sailed through the air, she, too, will set sail soon, decorating her real-world atmosphere with hope and boundless energy. In lucrative times or lean, she will climb into pantyhose, pumps and, depending on her circumstance, maybe even upgrade her beverage of choice from Boone's Farm to cherry Mad Dog 20/20.

But before she leaves her home of four years, one last tradition: "I'm streaking the lawn before the sun rises."

Longing for that straitjacket to climb into, I realize that, as she works to find a job, I've worked myself out of one.

A Brand All Her Own

"So, what does your son/daughter do?"

Over time, our answer to that question has ranged from "soccer" to "Keystone Light" to "if we're lucky, eight months with probation."

But now that our daughter has graduated from college and joined the ranks of income tax-paying capitalists, formerly known as "losers" and "parents," cocktail banter centers on this question.

"Oh, they're great!" other parents answer. "Prescott/Tiffany/Denzel is on Wall Street/Broadway/Oprah."

Then, they turn to me.

"My daughter?" I say. "Oh, she drives a truck and builds chip 'n dip displays at WalMart." Silence generally follows as they attempt to hide their mental dance in the end zone, having won the "Tell me about your kid, so I'll feel better about my own" game—which is like Mortal Kombat, only bloodier.

Clinging to the lowest rung of corporate America, our daughter now climbs out of bed at the same hour she used to climb into it, a rite of passage reserved for her management training program at, what sounds like, "Feed Olé." (I don't want to get sued, plus if her boss reads this and fires her, she might move back home.)

So, I answered one inquiring mind, "She works at Feed Olé."

"Really," he said, "the CIA!" Not even my looking stupid stopped him from firing questions I couldn't answer or imagining details of her covert ops.

When our daughter was engaged in the interviewing process and someone asked me what she did, I'd say vaguely, "At this point, she's not sure which end is up."

"What?" they'd ask. "She's signed up?"

"Why, yes. She's always loved playing in the mud and holding her breath underwater. She can hardly wait for her Navy SEAL training to begin."

"Well, sure," they'd say, dismissively. "If you're headed that way, I'd love another gin."

Our daughter, Liberal Arts degree in one hand and D.O.T. certification in the other, cruises across South Texas, the land of javelina roadkill, flyboys and red sky. Occasionally, she cruises home to refuel.

It's a strange sensation, having your grown child for dinner. She, who lives in another city, pays her own bills and has a 401K...something she thought just six months ago was a fun run.

No longer able to demand that she set the table, eat her vegetables and wash the dishes, I treat her like a real guest: if she needs anything, she has to get up and get it herself.

Talk consists of her route between Bulk and C-stores; weekenders and end caps; and sleeves—not packaging, but the density of tattoos on the arms of guys who hit on her as they eye her deftly moving her dolly.

She explains the difference between a hurricane and, say, Thanksgiving—the former being a chip "event;" the latter, a chip "holiday"...of which, she gets none.

And, my favorite, their highly complicated marketing strategy: people will bend over only for what they like.

I ask if I could quote her.

After dinner, she blows through our kitchen like a corporate raider, taking inventory of our pantry, chip drawer and cookie jar. I feel like a member of the French Resistance hiding the wrong brand of everything. "You people better start buying the right products! No more Nabisco! DO YOU HEAR ME?" she barks.

What her dad and I know about the corporate world could fill an empty chip bag. So, we stand by, waiting for the time she'll be fully vested, which used to mean a Banana Republic three-piece suit.

Jimmy Choo, Kate Spade and Burberry will have to wait. For now, she sports a kidney belt, chinos and bruises on her arms the size and color of eggplants.

So, it's not investment banking, software development or nuclear arms negotiations, but as she works her way across the bottom, taking neither a prime display location nor expiration dates for granted, her determination—and treating a C-store manager as though he was Sam Walton—well, such hard work and dedication would've inspired Dale Carnegie.

The only time I ever put in an 18-hour day, I was in labor, so she is hardly a chip off the old block. But I did manage to deliver, while not on time, a product who is a brand all her own.

East is Right

"Don't worry about me, mom," he said with an intense hug, the kind he gave when he was little, lasting long enough for me to feel its intensity, but not sink into.

Within moments, he was gone...disappearing into the chaos of travelers. His destination, his dream.

My nightmare?

It's a scene we've played many times—our saying "Be safe. Call us. Fly right." His asking, "What airline am I on? Where's my ticket? Do you have my passport?" Clueless, he'd wander off in the general direction of the plane—he, fueled with wonder of the world; me, wondering when in the world I'd ever see him again.

College now complete, he won't be gone for the summer or even a semester. With no plan and an open-ended return ticket from across the Atlantic, he's off to experience a worldly existence where there is no core curriculum, but years of electives with results uncertain. For now, his fate and occupation is to measure the world and see what his future holds.

Since his goal is to live a life of retirement, we told him that it helps to have a job first.

In a last-ditch effort to help him determine what he wants to be when he grows up, we offered aptitude tests—the same tests my father gave my old boyfriends. Digging beyond their flair for blowing smoke rings, shooting beers, coordinating dual flipped-up collars, and their SAT scores (can you say 700?), Dad hoped the tests might unearth hidden natural talents.

Silly Dad.

Fortunately, I married a guy who brought solid genes to the table: logical thinker, but wholly disorganized. So, when our son's testing indicated he'd stink at clerical work, he stated flatly, "I never wanted to be a priest, anyway."

Unfortunately, my genes passed on a void of spatial ability. Giving my son a map—which could come in handy when traveling—is like handing Michael Moore a guide to nutrition. Which explains why, when he has needed directions and his dad instructed, "Turn east," our son turned right. Even if he was headed south.

Packing for his "Where's Waldo" farewell tour, he stuffed all his itinerant needs into one backpack, moaning, "If only I'd designed a SAMP—Socially Acceptable Man Purse." With the backpack stitches bursting, he discarded nonessentials—underwear, deodorant, toothpaste—to make room for...a hot dog costume. What else do you wear to the World Cup?

"Pursue your passion," we'd always told him. I just had no idea that would take him to the Middle East. I guess he knew all along that, for him, East truly is right.

Viewing time from one end, it stretches to infinity. From the opposite end, you wonder where it went. I thought he'd be with us for my lifetime. It turns out that meant only a fraction of his.

Although some days were louder than others, we taught him all we knew. In return, we learned odds are good that he will lose his phone, his passport, his credit card and, when he jumps the tracks, probably even his way.

But in doing so, he will find himself.

Meanwhile, the pieces that have defined him thus far—his Bob Marley CDs, autographed baseballs, his dog and dog-eared history books, even his little sister—wait for him. Right where he left them.

Standing in the wings waiting to hear from him, I click my e-mail's inbox, minutes drifting by like an hourglass glued to the table. His blog carries snippets of his journey through the universe, some entries containing information hazardous to my health.

Half-hoping to catch a glimpse of him, I watch the World Cup through interlaced fingers. And I could swear that, sandwiched in between the Elvis impersonators and two babes wrapped in U.S. flags (and that's all), I see a hot dog waving into the camera mouthing, "Hi, Mom!"

The world is his oyster. Which reminds me...I wonder if he remembered his EpiPen®?

Soul's Compass

Most mothers and daughters, after being apart for some time, hug and kiss. Some raise eyebrows trying not to comment on new piercings, tattoos (the mother's), navy blue hair or deeper wrinkles (the daughter's).

My daughter and I greet one another like the Two Stooges—stinging high fives, vise-like pinches and maybe a love tap...with the goal being to trip one another.

Passersby have been known to calculate odds and solicit bets, throw a red card or maybe even turn a fire hose on us. Once our undying affection warms up, we grab. She might grab my neck in a half nelson; my hair, creating a necessary, but temporary, face-lift; or my knee with a crippling horse bite.

No longer as strong or as quick as she, these days I'm capable of grabbing only the check.

I'm not sure when this routine began. Maybe it was the first time she left for camp. Granted, camp was six weeks, a month longer than most. And it was a few states away. In the mountains. Near bears. And she was nine.

As we parted, she grabbed my neck. Or was it me who grabbed hers? In either case, I convinced her that she'd be fine...or was it she who convinced me?

Regardless, I convinced everyone that her being away, on her own, was a good thing.

Everyone. Honest.

Except the woman who lay in my bed each night with my covers pulled over her head...her tears in my ears.

As a teenager, my daughter left home one entire summer to build latrines in a remote Bolivian village. Living with no plumbing or electricity, she walked every morning to far corners, returning each night to sleep on a dirt floor.

Her cowboy hat strapped to her lone, bulging backpack, she had no room to pack the parting gift I'd bought her. As she turned to board the plane, she grabbed my hand—or did I grab hers? Whichever...I took from my pocket a small box and placed it in her hand.

Where she was going, having enough underwear, DEET™, and Imodium were a far grander concern than any stupid trinket I could offer.

But, over the course of her then-sixteen years, she had given me direction, decorating my life with her nonpareil, self-assured quintessence. Somehow my gift—tiny, working compass earrings that really worked—seemed fitting to decorate her life.

Not that they'd really help her find her way, as she had helped me, but maybe they'd help her find her way home.

Our lives became a series of goodbyes—college, studying abroad, her odyssey to find a job. Me, convincing everyone it was no big deal.

Everyone. Honest.

During rare emotional calls home, a knife slicing through her voice, I'd struggle to grab her, searching for the right words. Her mature voice slowly gaining control as she embraced the *inevitable this, too, shall pass*, I'd hang up in wonder—who, exactly, was consoling whom?

She's grown now. Living in a different city. Having reached, at last, the official age of self-sufficiency, she's on her own. But then, she'd convinced me long ago that she always had been. Or...?

Together last weekend, we caused a stir again. As we tortured one another at a ballgame with grabs, pokes and horse bites, the young couple behind us was torn—not knowing whether to discipline their own fighting kids or separate the two of us.

Last night, in her absence, I pulled back the covers of her bed. Her bed on the far end of the sleeping porch of our river house. Banked on one side is a wall of glass—beyond it, a blanket of stars. Although we're apart, we share the same night sky.

As I lay connecting the twinkling dots of silver peripatetic starlight, my soul's compass grabbed me.

That's our way now. Although, I wonder...who is grabbing whom?

Under the Bed

One would think that at my age, I no longer would fear monsters under the bed. But, on occasion, they are still there.

The first monster bared his teeth when I was five or six. My family had just returned home from a weekend trip. We unloaded the car, opened the mail and, while turning off various lights that had burned in our absence, we stopped cold—the patio door dangled from its hinges. Scattered around the threshold were wood fragments and shards of broken glass. Our home had been burglarized.

Despite my parents' and the policemen's assurances, I was certain it was monsters and one remained behind—under my bed. I told no one, knowing instinctively that if I was very, very quiet, and cautious not to rustle my covers, he would not find me. Not hear me breathless.

And so I lay the first brick of fear, followed by others, brick upon brick, until I'd constructed a wall blocking out the monster. Each night, I went to bed and said my prayers intently, before burrowing under my bedspread to tick off the minutes of another night alive.

Time afforded me a way of outgrowing the fear of that monster. But others took his place.

When my kids ran to me in the wee hours with tales of a monster under their bed, I was not surprised. I'd remind them of Max in *Where the Wild Things Are* who stilled the monsters, taming them with his special magic before he returned home where someone loved him best of all. I'd peer under their bed, as if that would prove he was not there. But we both knew I could not see him—he was not my monster. In my heart, I couldn't deny his existence. And, I knew, once I stepped from their room, he'd return.

The monsters of their childhood no longer haunt them.

But as they step into the real world, different monsters will roar their terrible roars and gnash their terrible teeth. A boyfriend who steals her heart; a girlfriend who manipulates him; a professor who imparts prejudice; an interviewer who cuts them off; the fear of failure, fear of success; fear of conforming, of not conforming; fear of becoming someone other than who you are. Monsters everywhere.

Still inclined to be very, very quiet, hiding under the covers of our conscience, we are inclined even as adults to build walls high enough and thick enough to hold the monsters at bay.

Behind walls, you can breathe. Under the covers, you lie safe. Or so you believe.

I try to reassure my children, just as I did when they were little, but I still cannot deny the monsters' existence. There will always be wild things waiting to grab you and pull you under, if you let them. My kids have yet to face the dictatorial boss, the IRS auditor, the bad lab report, the worse investment, or the teenager who fights back when you try to point out the right path.

I could try to declaw their monsters with an endless stream of words. Or I could teach my children how to build, not walls, but confidence and faith to walk through the fear, allowing its opaque fog to wash over them until they safely reach the other side...another day alive. Stronger for having done so.

We tell our children of our mistakes, our monsters, real and perceived, the ones we cannot control, the ones who control us; that we've lived over 50 years of another night alive. But they must learn some things on their own. As they become armed with their own special magic, they can embrace life's shifting sands and face their slow parade of fears.

Some nights I still burrow under the covers, but in the crook of The Bob's arm that I've come to know so well, I return home where someone loves me best of all. Safe, sound, another night alive.

Even now, after the kids are tucked in and safely asleep—either in my home or theirs miles away—I try to swathe them in enough love and support so that we will be able both to deal with and slay those unconscionable things under the bed.

And when the sun rises, armed with confidence, faith and knowledge that we have what it takes not only to confront them, but also live with them and overcome their existence, only then will we be truly alive.

Another day, another night. Thank God.

Momsense

It's not easy being a kid. They just want to have fun, but there's always some higher-up lurking over them, sniffing out danger in the safest of sandboxes—mothers.

Mothers are great for babies. One little smile from a new-born bundle makes a mother's eyes shine and her heart melt, leaving no question that the diapered set rules. Within months, however, the tides turn. Mothers start expecting stuff in return for their long hours: sit up, stand by yourself, take your first step; and, before you know it, the big one—ride a bike...with no training wheels. They tell you they won't let go, but they do. Just like Lucy with Charlie Brown's football—they always pull away. And, then, it's all over but the crying.

Any seasoned kid knows that life gets more confusing because mothers make no sense.

They make you wear sweaters when *they're* cold and take naps when *they're* tired. They cherish your tiny handprint in clay, but send you to your room when you finger-paint on the living room walls. They tickle you until you scream, but are disgusted if milk comes out of your nose. They plan coast-to-coast car trips with siblings you despise, knowing you'll get carsick before you leave your block.

They spank you, claiming it hurts them more than it does you, but you're the one sitting on a pillow. They love the freedom of holidays, but make you go to school. They tell you to just do your best but A's pay more, and to make new friends—just not with strangers.

They pray for all the starving children in the world, then try to kill you with poisonous vegetables. They demand conversation at the dinner table, but holler if you talk with food in your mouth. They believe Cokes are bad, unless you're sick, then they're good; and if you drink out of the milk jug, it's germ warfare—as if wiping your face with a Kleenex they've spit on is good hygiene.

They lecture on good sportsmanship, but scream when you run the wrong way down the field and threaten to slash the referee's tires when he makes a bad call. Anything you watch on TV is trash, but *All My Children* is educational.

They brag about you to their friends, then cast evil spells on you: "May *you* have children someday!" They look in the mirror, proclaiming proudly, "I am my kid's mom," but look at you and say "No...because I said so."

And this person is in charge of your self-esteem? *Will she ever let go?* One minute, she wishes you'd stay little forever, and the next she asks, "When are you going to grow up?" Then one day you do.

Only it gets worse. You turn into a teenager—dying for privacy and independence—and your mother turns into an investigative reporter, searching under your bed, through your drawers and in your pockets for evidence of, well, she's not sure, but she'll know it when she finds it.

She asks what you're doing behind closed doors when she already knows. She repeats a thousand times to pick up your room, quit holding your little sister's hair over the gas pilot, and to get off the phone—then looks stunned when you do.

She encourages you to invite friends over, then says they're the "wrong" crowd. She tells you to get a job and earn some money, when it'd be so much easier for her just to give you some of theirs.

She opens Pandora's box by discussing sex, alcohol and drugs, then tells you not to do it, drink it or smoke it. She frowns on "public displays of affection," then kisses you in front of all your friends...with lipstick on.

And you wonder, *Will she ever let go?*

Then one day she does—and reflected in your mirror is a whole person ready to go it alone. All the prying, prodding, picking and pestering haven't torn you apart; it's shaped you. It's given you wings and the courage to test them.

The madness of motherhood always will be a mystery to kids, dogs and husbands. But as a new mother, when you look at your own bundle and feel your eyes shine and heart melt, the madness doesn't seem mad at all. It's momsense.

You promise to love and protect and never let go, unless, of course, it's time for them to learn to walk, ride a bike or be a man. But first you'll say, "Put on a sweater. I'm cold."

Rearview Revelations

Now occupying a home where doors never slam, toilet seats stay down and CD players don't shake the walls, I feel safe that no one (that I know of...at this particular moment) is inebriated, indicted or incarcerated. As a spectator now, I relish their lives from afar, mindful that I'm only a cell phone call, text or e-mail message away—communications are rare, but they do come.

In this empty house, I leaf through the brittle, brown-edged photo albums chronicling their formative years and watch old home movies. I vaguely recall the little girl who hated dresses; the boy who wore his cowboy hat every day...and nothing else. And the baby who begged her dad to play dress-up, sit in the little chair across from her to sip tea...and he did.

I reflect on my wise and oh-so-intuitive predictions of my kids' futures. Some, way off mark. Others, spot on.

Our oldest may really be on her way to being a CEO. From warehouse level, she has stacked, cracked and called-back more

Frito Lay products than South Texas could possibly consume.

Those one-way conversations in which I used to fire off more questions than a talk show host hoping to stir conversation have been replaced with soulful, adult mother-daughter exchanges—the latest sale at J. Crew, the perfect heel height that enhances her legs...and cripples mine, the ingredients of the perfect man. But nothing compares with her passion for her job that often is reflected in late- night conversations—whether explaining the impact a shortage of corn has on the chip industry, a bean dip crisis or why I can't seem to buy the right brand soft drink.

When back in town—and out on it—she might call me long after my bedtime, coercing me to get dressed to meet her for a beer at a local dive with her friends. Beauty being that, now, it's not my credit card she's after... it's to share her stories, our laughter. Make more memories together.

My son, who as a tyke was ever ready for battle, is still armed. Having set down his childhood plastic weapons, he now wields a sword of passion and peace.

He has grown from living by the creed, "It's not whether you win or lose, but how you place the blame," to being a soldier for social justice; from never wanting to leave home to flying across the world, no return ticket in hand, to experience the world first-hand; from digesting history and religious theory to living in Africa for a year to aid in the education of orphans.

Peripatetically, he traverses the stars on his journey, immersing himself in his quest for earthly and godly answers. While separated by several hours, oceans and continents, I find solace that we are under a variation of the stars he wanted to give me so many years ago.

Possessing a writer's soul, he is now armed with words and a wit that could etch glass. The perfect revenge for a guy who grew up having to read about puberty—his own—as his mother updated readers on his latest chest-hair count.

And he would not forgive me if I did not mention that he will go to his grave believing that the Astros will win the World Series one day.

The youngest, the baby—the one who was drug around like a rag doll, hanging on for dear life as she clung to her older siblings' every move. The one whose siblings loved to torture, telling her she was a giant mistake. The one who, I feared, even though she was a happy camper, would never step into her own shoes, but be led by the nose...or serve as a doormat. She came into her own, growing into a wisdom beyond her years and finding a voice that is uniquely hers.

The day came when her brother and sister, performing their regular schtick, were peppering her with verbal flak. As they accused her of having, doing and getting away with more than they ever did, she turned to them and, using the quote from Erma Bombeck that served as the basis of my mothering, calmly said, "Children are like pancakes. You should throw the first two away."

She has spent all her years of wide-eyed silence observing, taking notes. Notes on how to overcome challenges with grace and humility. Notes on how to deal with people. Notes on how not to follow, but how to lead. And how to inspire.

It is she, the one left behind to fend for herself as the only child at home for eight years, who bathes my life with her smile and fills the house with laughter. It is she who teaches me by example, whose gut I trust more than my own.

During the closing ceremonies of her summer camp, her most treasured part of life, her cabin mates were drowning in tears, lost in saying goodbye to the closest version they will ever experience of Camelot. Reflective, but dry-eyed, she looked at me and said, "It's time to go."

Reading my quizzical silence, she continued, "Mom, if I don't let go of this chapter, I might miss the next."

Hardly a mistake, that one.

It is their turn now. Their turn to pay taxes, find their soul mate and, with luck, have kids just like them.

After their lifetimes of my telling them what to do, the last secret to motherhood rose up before me, to become as indelibly etched in my brain as their long-ago oil-based scribbling on my walls: Say nothing. Keep the light on, and a chair at the dinner table. And never, ever give up.

Based on my own U-turns in life, I know that any mistakes they make now will serve their future well. As Will Rogers said, "Good judgment comes from experience, and a lot of that comes from bad judgment."

As they continue to learn, this mother's continuing education continues.

In fertilizing these young shoots over the growing-up years of their lives, I realize that I am the one who has finally grown into who I am meant to be. As my roots delved deeper into the ground and my arms, my face and soul lifted heavenward, I faced the sun. And it surely did shine upon me. Even in dark times.

Those things I had hoped for them as little ones—have high IQs, watch PBS, score perfect SATs, be a B.M.O.C, get an MBA and drive BMWs—was wasted energy. They became who and what they are, not so much because of what I did, but because when they told me to "chill," I did. When they let me know it was time to let go, I did. And when they were ready to talk, laugh or cry, I was in lockstep.

As each new chapter of their lives unfolded, I learned bit by bit to get out of the way. After setting boundaries as my father advised, I found my children were not the only ones who found their way. And in learning from my youngest that if you don't let go of one chapter, you might miss the next.

Because it only gets better.

At last, I take time to smell the roses. These roses, who, as small buds, were showered with a salty combination of sweat and tears. Who, in dormant times, were pampered with encouragement and, when wilting against life's unfairness, propped up by a tender but stronger-than-I-realized shoulder. Whose thorny words, at times, provided a crown for this martyr mother, but, more often, provoked prickly glares. They were pruned with my mistakes and fertilized with dreams—mine, at first; now theirs.

Their perennial blossoms decorate my landscape with color and fragrance. New shoots growing every year, they branch out. I still water and feed them with infectious love, but now I sit back and watch the world lean over our fence to admire them for who and what they are. From my bloom with a view, on many days I wonder who raised whom.

After years of saying the wrong thing; being too harsh, too soft; straddling the beam between guilt and taking credit for things only fate controlled, my "Aha!" moment finally hit. Something other than a new life blossomed each time I pushed in that delivery room.

Each time, a child was given life...and as they grew, so did I. As they blossomed, so did I.

Little did I know that falling into motherhood did, in fact, involve falling apart, into enemy hands and to my knees praying for help. But the glorious exception was that I also fell into three magnificent pieces of good fortune.

In my reflection is the great revelation that, while I tried on several different lives over the years, I finally found the skin in which I am most comfortable. With the help of three insiders, I blossomed not only as a human being, but also as a mother.

If not for my children, I might never have known that it matters not when we bloom...only that we make it to the flower show.

In my garden there is a large place for sentiment. My garden of flowers is also my garden of thoughts and dreams. The thoughts grow as freely as the flowers, and the dreams are as beautiful.

—Abram L. Urban

The Last Word

By Bayless Parsley

Everyone always has the same reaction when I tell them my mom is a writer.

"A writer? How cool!"

And then,

"What does she write about?"

Every time.

It's a difficult question. At the root, the answer is, "My family." But that's leaving out a whole lot of commentary on my part. My mom does write about our family, true, but she has a way of describing us at times that leaves me yearning for a right of polite rebuttal.

Example No. 1: my dad does not introduce himself with a definite article attached to the front of his name. (But he does, thanks to my idea and my mom's initiative, drive a car with Texas vanity plates that say "THE BOB.")

Example No. 2: we Parsley kids do not speak like bumbling idiots, using words like "like" and "um" more than Emeril says "Bam!" Yes, we do say those words from time to time. But like, I don't know, space fillers are just like, ya know, part of like growing up in America or whatever. Ya know? It's not like we don't, like, know how to talk or something.

Example No. 3: I never finished a baseball season 0-15. That would just be embarrassing. The worst a team of mine ever did was 1-15, the Mustangs, my first year of teeball.

I will admit, though, that I did forget my passport when going to Jamaica. But not because I didn't know you needed one to leave the country. I just never actively thought about it until I was at the check in desk at Reagan National Airport. My passport was tucked into a drawer under my desk in Houston.

I can't remember how old I was when my mother began writing seriously. It was before I started being interested in girls, but after I stopped believing in Santa Claus. Somewhere safely between the eight and thirteen range. So it's safe to say that my childhood in Houston took place under the shadow of Louise Parsley's minor celebrity.

"I'm Bayless Parsley, nice to meet you."

Before the hand shake would end, almost every time, Joey Six Pack's mother would respond with, "Are you related to Louise Parsley?" I would nod. "Oh, I just loooove your mom's articles! She is just so great."

Have you seen the muffin tops "Seinfeld" episode when Kramer is trying to convince Jerry to help him promote his burgeoning "Real Peterman" tour? "Jerry, you're a minor celebrity. If you go on this thing, it could create a minor stir."

Minor stirs were always my mom's specialty.

I'll spare you the bullet points and just cut right to the quintessential example of her proclivity for making waves in my childhood public persona. It came around eighth or ninth grade, when my flower started to blossom, if you catch my drift.

I was a late bloomer. Not my fault. Completely out of my control. I gather from reading my mom's book, it's a genetic thing. Like The Bob being so tone deaf he'd leave his blinker on for the entirety of I-10, from sea to shining sea; like my sister Garland's curly fro making her look like John McEnroe as a child, thanks largely in part to the trips to SuperCuts financed by my mom; like recovering tomboy Elizabeth packing a punch harder than Mike Tyson to this day; or even like my mother's own teeth, which, when she sleeps at night, grind like a drunk sophomore at a high school homecoming dance, my God-given affliction was that I was the absolute last one of my friends to grow.

I remember the day I hit 5 feet. I was in eighth grade when I heard the good news in the doctor's office, after the obligatory weigh in/measurement routine which had never seemed to go my way. I was stoked. Five feet meant that one chapter of my life was about to close, and with it, the opening of another, about which I was extremely excited. The big 'P': puberty. Its absence in my own body had been an extremely sore subject around our house for some time. I had agonized over it. Yearned for it, like Jim-for-Pam yearning.

Every year, as I slowly inched my way closer and closer to the absolute first spot in line for the class yearbook photo, I began to suspect more and more that my mother had simply gotten lazy after my birth, her second in 14 months—what, had she just filled up my baby bottle with the leftover coffee every morning, rather than take the time to breast feed me like normal moms do with first born sons? Such a scenario wouldn't be such a stretch, really—this is the same woman who came home from the hospital with three-day-old Bayless in her arms only to find one-year-old Elizabeth out in the backyard doing somersaults, the natural reaction from a kid that age taking half a baby bottle full of scotch to the dome without remembering to eat first.

Anyway, I'm getting off topic. The kicker of this ultimate bullet point—the highlight of the long list of embarrassing things written about me during my childhood by my own mother—came when she announced to the world that her son, who remained nameless, (as if that would actually shield my identity from the devoted circle of ladies who are obsessed with Louise Parsley's "To Wit" columns), had "finally" started puberty.

Yeah. I know.

It wouldn't have been so bad had she not been a minor celebrity. But she was, and is—meaning that that line definitely created a minor stir, the ripple effects reaching all the way into my homeroom class, where the children of the devoted lady readers made sure to let me know that they'd read my mother's latest piece.

And I wonder why I retain a Napoleonic complex to this day, when, as my mom has told you, I measure in at an even six feet.

I can't speak to the most embarrassing moments for either of my sisters, or even for The Bob, because we've become extremely adept at simply blocking these events from our memories. But something tells me that nothing they could ever dredge up would compare to the horror unleashed within the psyche of an insecure, late-blooming 14-year-old kid whose entire class reads that he has just recently—"finally," to be exact—started puberty.

And yet...

And yet I wouldn't have had it any other way, looking back. My mother may have used us four for target practice, but at least we got some publicity out of it. And more importantly, we learned, perhaps subconsciously, the true meaning of "I am rubber and you are glue." I attribute my sense of humor to two overriding influences in this life of mine: "Seinfeld" and Louise Parsley, the minor celebrity capable of creating a minor stir, who also goes by the alias of "Bayless' mom." She taught me how to write—not by sitting me down and telling me which keystrokes to make, but by example. Or more importantly, through genetics. I am who I am because I am Louise's son. I am a writer, albeit, one whose celebrity is still years away from even reaching the status of "minor."

From my dad, The Bob, I've learned plenty of other things. I won't get into those now. This is my mother's book. And God knows we've been waiting for it for quite a while, and she deserves a little time in the sun. She hasn't had an easy draw in life. I'm not talking about financially, or even medically, although wearing corrective shoes until eighth grade probably wasn't much fun. I'm talking about the seminal event in her development into the person she is today: the early death of her father, "Grandfather Bayless."

That is what I call him; I never met him. None of us ever did. He died on an operating table at age 57, his heart refusing to pump any longer, when Elizabeth was just a bump on my mom's stomach. And I've always felt the hurt that lingers in my mother's bones to this day. His absence throughout my life has been almost tangible, the way you would think a man's presence should feel. I never met him, but I know him. James L. Bayless, by trade a stock broker, was in essence the original comedian in our family. The wit and humor that Houston's moms think to be the property of my mother, or her brother Jim, or myself, all traces back to the source: my grandfather. And it is through humor that I have come to know him.

"Your grandfather would get such a kick out of..."

Everything. Anything and everything I've done that has made my mom laugh, he would get a kick out of, she says. Her only son, her only dad. The two of us share the same eyes, an almost uncanny resemblance that lives on between my ears and the yellowed, black-and-white photographs that sit in frames throughout our home. But, from what I can glean from her stories—what he would "get such a kick out of"—we also share the same spirit, my grandfather and I. In a way, I feel like I represent a connection to his legacy in her eyes. And it is making my own eyes well up with tears to think about as I type these words.

My mother's essence is embodied in her writing. It is how she expresses who she is, who she was, and who she strives to become. The Bob always says he loves the way she writes because "she'll make ya laugh, she'll make ya cry." She doesn't make fun of us because she's looking for cheap laughs; she does it because it's how she expresses her love, as strange as that may sound to someone who comes from a household that was a little more...reverent. For her, life isn't as serious as it is for others. She'd rather live a short life filled with laughter than live a long one devoid of it. Kind of like her father did.

That is what I love most about my mother. That is what she writes about.